· WARD LOCK MASTER GARDENER ·

Lawn Craft

ALAN TOOGOOD

WARD LOCK

First published in Great Britain in 1993
by Ward Lock Limited, Villiers House, 41/47 Strand,
London WC2N 5JE, England
A Cassell Imprint

British Library Cataloguing in Publication Data
is available upon application to the British Library

ISBN 0 7063 7103 8

Text filmset by DP Press, Sevenoaks
Printed and bound in Singapore

Previous page: **Two circular
lawns. This shape is an
ideal way to make a narrow
garden appear much wider.**

Page 4: **Lawns can be
'furnished' with
ornamental specimen trees.**

Contents

Preface

The idea of an area of grass for leisure and decorative purposes, what we now call a lawn, dates from the fourteenth century. Yet it is amazing that there are so few books on the subject, although gardening magazines tend to cover lawns and their maintenance at least once a year.

Because of the relatively few books compared to other aspects of gardening, there tends to be a certain amount of mystery surrounding lawn craft. But the subject is straightforward enough, as revealed in the following pages.

As the lawn is generally the central feature in a garden, and indeed the design of the garden is often influenced by the lawn, the design aspects have been covered in perhaps greater detail than is found in other currently available books on lawns. However, as *Lawn Craft* is part of an essentially practical series, the practical aspects are covered in equally great detail.

To have a high-quality lawn that looks good all year round, you need to put in a fair amount of time on care and attention. In fact, it is fair to say that a lawn is one of the most labour-intensive features of a garden, comparable only to vegetable growing or greenhouse gardening.

With the following information at your fingertips, the hours you spend and the effort you make on producing a first-class lawn will be amply rewarded.

A.T.

ACKNOWLEDGEMENTS

The publishers are grateful to the following for granting permission to reproduce the following colour photographs: Tania Midgley (p. 1); Jerry Harpur (pp. 4, 8 & 17); Photos Horticultural Picture Library (pp. 9, 16 (lower), 48, 49, 60, 69, 72, 73, 80 (lower), 81 & 84); Harry Smith Horticultural Photographic Collection (pp. 12, 13, 16 (top), 20, 77, 80 (top) & 85); Pat Brindley (pp. 21 & 57); Atco Qualcast Ltd (p. 41); Hayters plc (p. 44); Amateur Gardening magazine (pp. 45 & 61); Fisons Horticultural plc (p. 53); and Royal Horticultural Society, Wisley (p. 76).

The photographs on pp. 24, 25, 28, 29, 32, 36, 37, 56, 64, 68, 88 & 89 were taken by Ed Gabriel.

The line drawings were drawn by Nils Solberg and Vana Haggerty F.L.S.

• 1 •

Shapely Ideas

Although the word lawn is not recorded before 1674, and the modern meaning of a closely cut covering of grass not until 1733, areas of grass or turf have been used as decorative features and for tournaments and games in gardens since the fourteenth century. Cutting of these early lawns was done with a scythe, but the practice was revolutionized in 1830 by the invention of the lawnmower.

It is generally accepted that a lawn is one of the most important features of many gardens today and indeed often influences the overall design. Many gardeners will design a lawn in conjunction with the rest of the garden.

But why is a level or slightly undulating expanse of green so important to many gardeners? Firstly, a lawn very much helps to create a sense of space in a garden and for this reason is often the central feature.

A well-designed garden should consist of a combination of open space, dense planting (say in beds and borders), vistas or long views, and areas hidden from view ('secret gardens'). This combination ensures an interesting garden full of surprises, yet without a claustrophobic atmosphere or 'shut-in' feeling.

A lawn can be and often is used to create the open space as well as vistas. However, it should be said at this stage that a lawn is not always a practical proposition in all gardens. Many modern, and not-

so-new gardens are very tiny, often called pocket-handkerchief gardens, and a lawn in such a plot would obviously be heavily used and could, therefore, soon become 'threadbare'. In this situation the owner has to think carefully whether or not a lawn is the best idea. A better option might be paving or gravel to create the open space.

What can a lawn offer?
• It creates a sense of open space.
• It is ideal for setting off other plants in beds and borders. The plain uniform green helps to act as a foil for stronger colours.
• A lawn helps to create contrast in a garden by providing another texture.
• It is a place for play and for outdoor living.
• Being green, it provides a very restful area.

SELECTING THE SITE

What points need to be considered when selecting a site for a lawn? The area needs to be chosen carefully for its suitability for the growing of grass. If badly chosen and conditions are not ideal, you will never have a good-quality lawn. It needs to be in an open position which receives a reasonable amount of sun. Deep shade, such as caused by trees with very dense canopies, will give problems, such as weak thin grass which is easily invaded by mosses. The site also needs to be well drained as a good lawn

7

◄ **This serpentine lawn is suitable for a long narrow garden as it creates the illusion that the plot is wider. It could also be used for linking different areas.**

► **A lawn must be sited in an open position which receives a reasonable amount of sun if it is to grow strongly and create a really dense sward.**

can never be achieved if the land regularly becomes very wet or waterlogged. The lawn is liable to become very muddy in wet conditions, even with normal use.

It was mentioned earlier that a lawn can be either completely level or slightly undulating. The latter is quite attractive as it creates more interest, so do not think that a perfectly level site is mandatory. However, the site should not slope more than 1 in 85 in any direction or mowing will become difficult. It must be mentioned here, though, that an undulating lawn is really only recommended for the larger garden, where it looks in proportion to the rest of the land: indeed, the land may be naturally undulating. In a small plot an undulating lawn appears far too fussy and even looks slightly ridiculous.

A question often asked is, 'What size should a lawn be?' The answer is that it should be in proportion with the other elements of the design. If too small it looks ridiculous, and if too large it will overpower the planting schemes. A good rule-of-thumb when designing a garden is to devote about a quarter to one-third of the site to the lawn.

SHAPES AND THEIR EFFECTS

The shape of a lawn must be considered extremely carefully. Often it dictates the overall design of the garden, more so with a small garden than with a larger one. Shape can also help to create the illusion that a garden is more spacious than it really is and one should, therefore, consider this aspect very carefully, especially if you have only a small plot.

Formal

There are several formal or geometric shapes that can be used for lawns such as square, rectangular, circular, or wedge shape where the lawn tapers from wide to narrow.

Although formal shapes are often used in small gardens where the overall design is symmetrical, you should be very wary of having, say, a square or rectangular lawn in a tiny garden of the same shape, as the effect will be to make the garden look even smaller. Avoid the common mistake of having a square or rectangular lawn in the centre of a garden of the same shape which results in straight narrow borders on either side. Better for a small garden would be an informal lawn, with gently curving or flowing edges, as described later.

Formal lawns, and indeed formal design in general, are easier in and perhaps more appropriate to larger gardens. Often, formality is reserved for the part of the garden nearest the house, and the design gradually merges into informal garden, perhaps including long-grass and wild-life areas.

So, for example, a formal garden near the house might feature a large square or rectangular lawn, with flower beds, perhaps including rose beds, of geometrical shape set in or around it, and maybe a formal pool with fountain. Adjacent to the house there may be a patio, or perhaps a raised terrace with steps, leading onto the lawn.

Many gardens are long and narrow and here various formal shapes can be used to make them appear wider than they really are. Circles are particularly useful. A series of interlocking circles the width of the garden is a possibility (Fig. 1). The circle nearest the house could be a patio, and the next one or two could be lawns. Any number of circles may be used in the overall design, of course: it all depends on the length of the garden. Avoid at all costs the common mistake of a series of small circles set in the middle of the plot – you need to make full use of the width for this idea to be really effective.

Alternatively you could consider the diagonal approach in your design if you have a long narrow garden. This will ensure the eye is taken across the plot rather than down the length of it. It also creates a sense of movement, and again will give the illusion that the garden is much wider than it really is.

The diagonal approach can be created with a zigzag lawn, with abrupt alternate left and right turns, if you want formality (Fig. 2). Again, as with circles, the lawn should extend from one side of the garden to the other. This design will create attractive triangular-shaped beds for planting. It will also ensure some long views or vistas, which create a sense of distance.

If you have a small garden, especially if it is square, why not consider a wedge-shaped lawn? This can give the impression of greater length. The widest part should be nearest the house, say

Fig. 1 Circles are useful for making a long narrow garden appear wider than it really is. A series of interlocking circles consisting of lawn and patio, the width of the garden, have been used in this design.

Fig. 2 The diagonal approach to design will also make a long narrow garden appear wider, and this can be achieved with a zigzag lawn. This design creates attractive triangular-shaped beds for planting.

A formal lawn is more appropriate to a larger garden and is generally sited near the house.

leading on from the patio, and perhaps the entire width of the garden. It should then taper uniformly to the end of the garden, where it will be much narrower, maybe only half as wide as the house end. Set a focal point of some kind at the end, as described later, and you really will create the illusion of greater length.

Informal

An informal lawn does not have a definite shape. It is irregular, with sweeping, 'flowing' or gently curving edges. It is easy to incorporate into a garden and suitable for all sizes, from the tiny pocket-handkerchief to one of several acres. Informal lawns can be used anywhere in a garden and are suitable for town, semi-rural and country gardens.

The great value of an informal lawn is that it can make a garden appear larger than it really is by creating the illusion of space. This applies particularly to small square or rectangular plots.

What shapes should you go for when planning an informal lawn? For small square gardens perhaps shapes that roughly resemble a large S, the figure eight or perhaps a kidney. However, you do not necessarily have to think of definite shapes, as the drawings on p. 11 illustrate.

As with formal lawns, you can also use diagonal designs to make a long narrow plot appear wider than it really is. This will, again, ensure movement

12

from one side of the plot to the other, rather than down the length. The design, aided by focal points, will also draw the eye from side to side.

An informal diagonal design can be created with a serpentine lawn, curving from one side of the plot to the other, rather like a snake. Note that the lawn should be made the full width of the plot – avoid at all costs a thin ribbon of serpentine lawn down the centre or it will make the garden look even narrower. A serpentine lawn will result in some attractively shaped planting areas on each side of the plot.

The plot shape that seems to give gardeners most problems when it comes to planning is the triangle. Forget about formality here and instead go for a design of irregular shape as this will help to make the plot look wider. An informal lawn could be created in the widest part of the plot to make this part look even wider. The narrow part of the plot, where it ends in a point, could be screened off, say with trellis. This could incorporate an arch, through which one enters the 'secret garden' that has been created.

Informal lawns are generally very suitable for large private gardens. Indeed, large formal gardens are not very often created these days, informality and natural gardening being very much more popular.

In big gardens there may be several large lawns with boldly curving edges, in various parts, each hidden from the other by plantings of tall shrubs and other plants, and these are often linked with broad 'flowing' grass paths, rather like green rivers meandering through the garden. Bold plantings are generally created on each side of the paths: perhaps flowing drifts of ground-cover plants such as heathers.

Gently undulating lawns are more of a practical proposition in large gardens and there is no doubt they look very attractive.

PATHS AND EDGINGS

Very often when planning a garden one needs to consider paths in conjunction with lawns. It is not generally advised that a path leads directly on to a lawn, otherwise the grass in that area will suffer from heavy use, becoming threadbare and with the ground compacted and muddy. Besides, a path should lead to something more definite: say a seat, a summerhouse or garden shed, a vegetable plot, pool, etc.

Having said that, it initially appears contradictory to allow a patio to lead direct on to a lawn, yet this is often advocated. However, the wear and tear on the lawn, where the two meet, is not so severe as access to the lawn is spread over a wider area.

Paths can be difficult to incorporate pleasingly into a garden. Try running a path along the edges of the lawn.

Access to a lawn, then, should not be very restricted if wear and tear are to be avoided.

A good idea is to design a path so that it runs along one edge of a lawn, along several edges or even completely around it, depending on requirements. This can be achieved whether the lawn is formal or informal. This technique does, in fact, make good design a lot easier in the informal situation.

The surface of a path should be lower than the lawn so that it does not foul the lawnmower. In any case, it is a good idea to allow a bare mowing edge or strip between the lawn and path, free from grass. Then the mower can be taken right up to the edge.

Do not use loose materials such as pea shingle, gravel or stone chippings for path making near a lawn as these have the habit of finding their way on to the lawn and fouling the mower. Instead, use concrete paving slabs, natural stone paving or paving bricks.

It is rarely pleasing aesthetically to run a solid path across a lawn, except perhaps in extremely large gardens where splitting a lawn in this way is not particularly noticeable.

If you want solid access across a lawn then by all means use stepping stones. These can, in fact, look most attractive set in a lawn. They will ensure dry access across the lawn in all weathers as well as preventing a track being worn. It is essential that the stones are set below ground level otherwise they will make mowing difficult.

Do not use square slabs for stepping stones as for some reason they do not look particularly attractive. Round or hexagonal slabs are a much better choice. The stones should be set so that you can walk easily and normally – you should not have to make huge strides or un-natural movements when using stepping stones! The stones look better if they are not set in a straight line. Instead allow them to meander across the lawn.

> **• HANDY TIP •**
>
> Trees and other plants growing in lawns should not have grass right up to the stems as this will retard growth. Instead leave a circle of bare soil, about 1 m (3 ft) in diameter. This should be kept free from weeds.

Edgings

A grass-free mowing edge or strip has already been mentioned above in relation to paths. This should, in fact, extend all round a lawn, as grass should never be allowed to grow hard up against things like walls, fences, etc, as it's then difficult to cut.

The strip not only makes mowing easier but ensures you can maintain neat edges with a pair of edging shears or a nylon-cord trimmer. It can be approximately 15 cm (6 in) wide.

There are various materials available which reinforce lawn edges and prevent them from being trodden down. Metal or plastic lawn-edging strip is quite popular and should be inserted slightly below the lawn surface.

NOT ALL GRASS

Lawns are not always simply bare expanses of grass – they may be 'furnished' with other things. For instance, focal points are often used in lawns. These may be living focal points such as trees, shrubs, conifers and bold perennials; or artificial like statuary, decorative plant containers and even garden seats.

A focal point is usually positioned at the end of a vista or long view and draws you to that particular part of the garden. For instance, a focal point may be sighted at the far end of a lawn, in the corner of a lawn, where a lawn changes direction – as in zigzag and serpentine lawns, or in the middle of a circular lawn.

· SMALL–MEDIUM FASTIGIATE TREES FOR LAWNS ·

Name	Description
Betula pendula 'Fastigiata'	Upright form of the common silver birch; white bark, deciduous foliage
Ginkgo biloba 'Fastigiata'	Columnar form of the maidenhair tree; deciduous; two-lobed, fan-like leaves turn yellow in autumn
Juniperus communis 'Hibernica'	Irish juniper; forms dense, dark green, prickly column
Juniperus scopulorum 'Skyrocket'	Very narrow; dark bluish-green evergreen foliage
Malus 'Van Eseltine'	Ornamental crab with upright habit; pale pink and white semi-double flowers in spring, followed by yellow fruits
Prunus 'Amanogawa'	Very narrow; wreathed from top to bottom in spring with clusters of scented, pale pink, semi-double flowers
Prunus 'Spire'	Another cherry with a very narrow habit, producing soft pink flowers and superb autumn foliage colour
Robinia pseudoacacia 'Pyramidalis'	A spineless and very erect form of the common acacia, with deciduous pinnate foliage
Sorbus aucuparia 'Fastigiata'	Pinnate leaves and big bunches of large orange-red berries in autumn

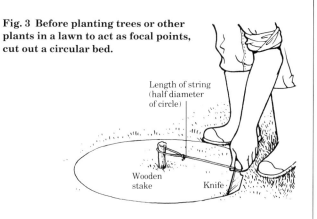

Fig. 3 **Before planting trees or other plants in a lawn to act as focal points, cut out a circular bed.**

Length of string (half diameter of circle)

Wooden stake

Knife

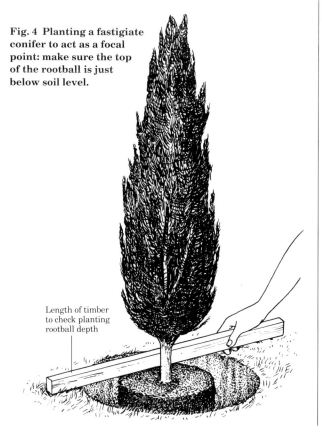

Fig. 4 **Planting a fastigiate conifer to act as a focal point: make sure the top of the rootball is just below soil level.**

Length of timber to check planting rootball depth

Living focal points

Specimen or single trees are often used as focal points in lawns. However, great care must be taken when choosing trees for lawns as many create deep shade and so prevent the grass from growing below them. Large spreading trees with dense crowns like beeches and oaks are typical examples. These may be all right in very large gardens and estates where bare soil below them is hardly noticeable, but they should definitely not be used in small lawns.

Instead choose small to medium fastigiate trees with a narrow columnar shape (see chart above and Figs. 3 and 4). Various deciduous kinds as well as

15

Specimen trees are often used as focal points in a garden and can be sited in a lawn.

Cortaderia selloana – the pampas grass is a favourite plant for use as a lawn specimen.

evergreen conifers fit the bill. These cast no shade to speak of and so the grass will not be affected. Also, the distinctive shape makes them ideal for use as focal points.

Certain perennials with a bold or distinctive habit of growth are also often used as focal points in lawns. Immediately coming to mind is the pampas grass, *Cortaderia selloana*, a large plant with widely arching foliage and, in late summer and autumn, 2.4 m (8 ft) tall plumes of feathery silvery flowers. There are also smaller, more compact cultivars such as 'Pumila'. However, pampas grass is really only suitable for the larger lawn due to its wide-spreading foliage.

Phormium tenax or New Zealand flax also makes an excellent lawn specimen with its erect evergreen

Lawns often create a vista or long view. A focal point is needed at the end to drawn the eye to this part of the garden. Statuary is often used for this purpose.

sword-like leaves. Try tall cultivars – 2.4 m (8 ft) – like cream-striped 'Variegatum' or light purple 'Purpureum'. For small lawns there are many small and dwarf cultivars available.

Yuccas are highly distinctive evergreen shrubs with bold sword-like leaves and spikes of cream or white lily-like flowers when established, making ideal focal points. Choose species like *Y. filamentosa*, height and spread 1 m (3 ft); *Y. gloriosa*, height and spread 1–2 m (3–6 ft); and *Y. recurvifolia*, of similar size.

Artificial focal points

• *Statuary* is popular for use as focal points and can create a romantic atmosphere in a garden. It is available in stone, reconstituted stone, bronze, lead and fibreglass. The more you pay the better the quality and the more satisfying the piece. There are human figures, animals, birds and abstract works. The latter are more in keeping in ultra-modern gardens, while human figures, animals and birds look at home in both town and country gardens. White or light-coloured statuary shows up best and gives a sense of distance, but it needs a dark background.

• *Urns and vases* in classical styles make excellent focal points in both formal and informal gardens. They vary enormously in size so are suitable for all gardens. They're available in 'warm' terracotta as well as light-coloured simulated stone. When used as focal points, ornamental containers do not have to be planted.

Urns and vases are ideal for siting in the centre of circular lawns, for example, as are sundials and stone bird-baths, also very popular for creating focal points.

● *Seats* The lawn is the ideal place for a garden seat, which again can also serve as a focal point. A white-painted seat would show up particularly well. A cast-iron or imitation one in traditional style would look good in a country garden. There are plenty of modern styles available for more formal gardens. A seat should ideally be backed by a hedge or wall to emphasize it. Wooden furniture – or even ornaments, in the form of carved tree trunks and wood sculptures – can be very appealing. Many rustic seats and tables are available, as well as more contemporary designs.

Statuary, containers and other items should be cemented onto a concrete paving slab set just below lawn level, this in turn being bedded onto mortar. It must, of course, be absolutely level. A garden seat will need a solid base longer and wider than itself to prevent it sinking in and the grass being worn. Again, this can be made from concrete paving slabs. Allow plenty of width at the front for feet and bed all the slabs on mortar.

Island beds

Lawns are ideal places in which to grow ornamental plants. They can be displayed in island beds, an idea that makes a refreshing change from traditional straight borders.

Try if possible to have a group of beds rather than one, with grass paths between them. A group of three beds looks good. The paths should be quite wide – certainly a minimum of 1 m (3 ft) if possible.

If space is limited it would be better to have just one large bed rather than two or three very small ones, which are inclined to result in a rather fussy appearance.

Island beds can be of regular shapes if you have a formal garden. But more generally today the trend is towards informality and so beds of irregular shape, with gently curving edges, are often used.

So what kinds of plants can be grown in island beds? They are excellent for hardy perennials, using self-supporting, but not necessarily all dwarf kinds. This will cut out the time-consuming chore of staking. They should provide colour from spring to autumn, with the display peaking in summer.

Some of the most spectacular summer island beds contain annuals, either mixed with perennials, or on their own. Annual flowers, which are generally at their most colourful in mid-summer, are either half-hardy (sown in spring with the aid of some heat), or hardy (sown – again in spring – straight outside). However, in fairness, although they can be extremely colourful, annual island beds are very labour intensive.

When planting island beds with perennials you must take into consideration their heights so that all can be seen when fully grown. The tallest plants – even some self-supporting perennials can reach 1.5–2 m (5–6 ft) – should be set in the centre of the beds, grading down to shorter ones at the edges. However, do not be too rigid in this respect, as it can create an unnatural, regimented appearance. Instead take a few groups of taller plants towards the edge, and a few groups of shorter plants towards the centre.

The plants should be arranged in bold irregular shaped groups of each kind. Each group can contain, say, three or five plants, or more, depending on the size of bed.

Of course, there are various other kinds of plants that can be grown in island beds. How about a collection of ornamental grasses? These can create quite a dramatic effect. As with hardy perennials, grasses range from dwarf to tall kinds.

Large-flowered and cluster-flowered roses are often grown in beds set in lawns. They are ideal for formal beds, but can also be grown in more informal situations.

Bulbs in short grass

Lawns that are regularly mown make excellent homes for various kinds of bulbs. A popular way of growing them is in bold drifts around and under specimen trees. Trees that are recommended for lawns do not cast dense shade, so bulbs, as well as the grass, will grow well underneath.

However, bulbs can be grown in other parts of the lawn, too. But bear in mind that the grass cannot be cut until the bulbs' foliage has completely died down to the ground. So do not have drifts of bulbs in 'inconvenient' parts of the lawn, such as slap bang in the middle! Instead, plant drifts, say, in the corners or along the edges of the lawn, where the long grass will not cause any problems, nor indeed look too conspicuous.

The word 'drifts' has been used advisedly, for bulbs in lawns should never be grown in formal groups, but instead in natural-looking irregular groups (Fig. 5).

The best bulbs for short grass are the dwarf-growing kinds, rather than tall bulbs like large-flowered daffodils that are better grown in flower and shrub borders. Their large foliage flops all over the place and is inclined to smother grass.

Possibly the most popular dwarf bulbs for lawns are the large-flowered Dutch crocuses with their goblet-shaped flowers in early spring. They come in various colours including yellow, blue, purple and white. Crocuses need a position in full sun for their flowers to open. Some crocus species can be grown, too, like *Crocus thommasinianus* whose funnel-shaped purple, lilac or violet flowers appear in the spring. The autumn-flowering *C. speciosus* can also be recommended. It produces light purple-blue flowers.

Other bulbs that can be recommended for lawns include chionodoxas or glory-of-the-snow, with their starry blue and white flowers in spring, and miniature scillas, also with blue star-shaped flowers. Both of these will grow in dappled shade or in full sun.

Provided you can give them a cool position with dappled shade, and soil which does not dry out, galanthus or snowdrops are ideal for naturalizing in lawns, particularly around trees. All have white flowers marked with green, and flower in winter or early spring.

Fig. 5 Scattering crocus corms over the ground and planting them where they fall creates a natural-looking drift.

SOMETHING DIFFERENT

The following covers difficult situations for grass and alternatives to the closely mown lawn – indeed, alternatives even to grass.

Banks

Many people, on taking over a new garden, find that it contains a steep bank. The immediate reaction is to grass it, to prevent soil erosion.

But is grass the best answer? Regular cutting will be necessary to keep it short, as this will look neater than long grass. Remember that cutting will be difficult if the bank is very steep. You will have to use a nylon-cord trimmer as you should never attempt to use a hover mower on a steep bank as it can be dangerous.

A grass bank can be boring, too: it can look too 'municipal'. Also, it can be difficult initially to grass a steep bank. You cannot carry out normal soil preparation, seeding is out of the question as grass seed can be washed away by rain, and turf, which is the recommended method, will have to be pegged to hold it in place until it has rooted into the soil.

So what's the alternative to grass? Low-growing ground-cover plants, with a dense, spreading, ground-smothering habit of growth. Refer to a specialist book on the subject for examples, such as *Ground Cover Plants* by Janet Browne, in the Concorde Gardening Series (Ward Lock).

Long-grass areas

Wild-flower gardening is becoming quite popular today and one aspect of this is the wild-flower meadow. It consists of an area of long grass with wild flowers growing in it. These attract various insects like butterflies, bees, hoverflies and grasshoppers.

Non-flowering chamomile forms a pleasing springly lawn and is fragrant when walked on or after a shower of rain.

It can, if desired, be an extension of the closely mown lawn, with which it will contrast pleasingly, or it may be created towards the end of the garden, perhaps in association with other wildlife habitats like a pond, woodland, cornfield and natural hedge.

It is best to buy from a specialist seedman a properly balanced grass seed and wild-flower mixture to suit your type of soil and the climate. The wild flowers must be indigenous to the area, otherwise they may not attract insects. It is never successful trying to turn an existing lawn into a wild-flower meadow – not only would sowing of wild-flower seed be difficult, but the lawn grasses would not be suitable as they are too vigorous and would smother the wild flowers.

Invariably the grasses used in mixtures also produce attractive flowers.

The site for a wild-flower meadow should be open and sunny. However, it must also be sheltered from the wind, as a windy site will deter insects.

◄ **Plants can be displayed in island beds set in a lawn.**

Very shady areas

A question often asked by garden owners is, 'Can a lawn be grown in shade?' The answer is, it depends on the density of the shade. In light shade, such as that created by tall buildings or screens with the site open to the sky, all grasses that are used for lawns should grow reasonably well. A presentable lawn is also possible in the dappled shade of small trees which have a light canopy of foliage. In each case a shade-tolerant grass-seed mixture should be used.

The heavier the shade the more difficult it becomes to establish a lawn. The most difficult situation is found under large trees with heavy canopies like oaks and beeches which create very deep shade – grass will not grow here. Also, the ground is likely to be poor and dry, again not suitable for the growth of grass. In these conditions it may be better to plant highly tolerant shade-loving ground-cover plants.

· TOUGH GROUND-COVER PLANTS ·

The following tolerate deep shade and poor dry soils, so are ideal substitutes for grass under large trees.

Name	Description
Butcher's broom (*Ruscus aculeatus*)	Evergreen shrub with dark green spiny stems and red berries (plant male and female plants)
Common ivy (*Hedera helix* cultivars)	Evergreen shrubs with plain or variegated leaves
Crane's bill (*Geranium macrorrhizum*)	Perennial with aromatic foliage and, in summer, pink or white flowers
St John's wort (*Hypericum calycinum*)	Deciduous shrub with large yellow flowers in summer
Yellow archangel (*Galeobdolon luteum* 'Variegatum')	Evergreen perennial with silver-splashed leaves and yellow flowers (rampant)

· HANDY TIP ·

It is not a good idea to subject chamomile, thyme and mint lawns to very heavy use as these plants are not as tough as lawn grasses. In this situation it would be wise to run stepping stones through the lawn.

Alternatives to grass

Lawns can be created from plants other than grass. For instance, delightfully fragrant lawns or even paths can be made from plants that have aromatic foliage such as creeping chamomile, thymes and mints. When trodden on, the foliage of these carpeting plants releases its scent. These lawns are intended as small decorative features in gardens and not for regular use.

The chamomile used for lawns does not produce flowers and is botanically known as *Anthemis nobilis* 'Trenegue'. It forms a very pleasing springy lawn, deep green in colour, which is especially fragrant after rain. It has a creeping habit of growth, the horizontal stems rooting into the soil as they grow.

The site for a chamomile lawn must be chosen carefully, for the plant needs a position in full sun with very well-drained soil. Light sandy soil is preferred. At all costs avoid wet soils and shade.

The carpeting thymes need the same growing conditions as chamomile. One of the best species to grow as a lawn is *Thymus serpyllum* with a prostrate carpeting habit, minute grey-green leaves, and tiny flowers in summer. Usually cultivars of this are grown, with red, pink, mauve or white flowers.

A mint with a suitable carpeting habit is *Mentha pulegium* (pennyroyal) whose tiny leaves smell of peppermint and which produces mauve flowers in summer. It needs to be grown in soil which retains moisture and will succeed in sun or partial shade.

• 2 •
Greening up the Land

When one is perfectly happy with the design of a lawn one can get down to the business of creating it.

Basically there are two ways of creating lawns with grass: by sowing grass seeds and laying turves.

• *Seed* The cheapest method is to sow grass seeds. Normally mixtures of several different grasses are used, chosen to suit your particular conditions and/or requirements.

Apart from cost, what are the other advantages of creating a lawn from seed compared to turfing? It is possibly true to say that you have a wider choice of mixtures for various purposes and conditions, although there is now a far wider range of turf available than was previously the case.

Grass seed is very much easier to handle than turves as it is light in weight. It is certainly a lot quicker to sow a given area with grass seed. You can choose a day when soil conditions and the weather are ideal.

Disadvantages of creating lawns from seed are that they take longer to establish and it can be at least a couple of months before you can start using the lawn. There are only two comparatively short periods in the year when grass seed can be safely sown.

• *Turf* What are the advantages of turf? It enables you to create a lawn quickly, and this can be used immediately. Laying turves is easy for many people.

Today, there is a wide choice of turf available for different conditions and uses. Turf can be laid during much of the year, the main period being autumn, winter and into early spring.

Disadvantages are that for some people turves can be heavy to handle, although there is now available lightweight turf that does not carry soil. Turves have to be laid soon after delivery, whatever the weather or soil conditions.

Here, then, is all you need to know about preparing the site and creating a lawn from seed and turf. Plus, grassing banks, creating a long-grass area, establishing chamomile and thyme lawns and planting bulbs in grass.

SITE PREPARATION

The very first step in site preparation is to transfer your lawn design to the actual ground. In other words, you will have to mark out accurately the shape of the proposed lawn.

Although it may sound contradictory, it is much easier to mark out an informal lawn, one of irregular shape with sweeping, 'flowing' or gently curving edges. All you need is one or several lengths of either hosepipe or rope. Or use some similar and easily available alternative.

This is then laid on the ground to the shape required. It can either be pegged in place, which is the ideal method, or the outline marked with sand

or by scoring the soil with a pointed stick and the pipe/rope taken up.

Formal lawns have to be marked out really accurately, otherwise they will look odd. For square or rectangular lawns, you will need a right-angled wooden frame to ensure you get the corners square. Use three pieces of straight-edged wood in an aggregate of 3:4:5 and join them together so that they form a triangle, one corner of which is a right-angle (90°). The shape can be marked out with short wooden pegs and white string.

A circle can be marked out by using a fixed stake with a length of string loosely looped over it. The length of the string should be half the required diameter of the circle. Attach a pointed stick to the other end and, with the string held taut, pull the stick around the stake, at the same time scratching a circle in the soil (Fig. 3 on p. 15). This can be emphasized with sand.

Clearing the site

Start preparing a lawn site at least two to three months in advance of sowing or turfing.

If you are faced with a new site, you may first have to clear away builders' rubble such as bricks, lumps of concrete and sand. These materials should not be dug into the soil as this can result in patchy growth of the grass.

If any trees have been removed from the site, make sure you dig out the stumps, plus any large roots near to the surface.

Kill off any perennial weeds by spraying them when in full growth with a weedkiller that contains glyphosate. Follow the manufacturer's instructions on use.

If the builders have removed all the topsoil, you will have to buy some in and spread it over the site once the weeds have been eradicated. A lawn site needs at least 15 cm (6 in) of topsoil and it should be of an even depth to ensure uniform growth of the grass. A medium to light loam topsoil is recommended.

◄ Although it may seem difficult to mark out the site for an informal lawn, it is probably easier than marking out a formal area – simply indicate the outline with rope.

▶ Levelling the lawn site, using wooden pegs and a spirit level. Minor levelling can be done with the topsoil, as here, major alterations with the subsoil.

Levelling

If you need to level the site it would be better to do so before adding topsoil. If you have to carry out major earth-moving it is best first to remove any topsoil and to level the subsoil. Then it can be replaced.

First, decide on the level required then hammer in a wooden peg at that point. It should protrude 10 cm (4 in) above the ground. Next, working from this 'master peg' insert more wooden pegs all over the site, 1.8 m (6 ft) apart. Insert them in a square grid system. The tops of all the other pegs must be level with the top of the master peg, and this is

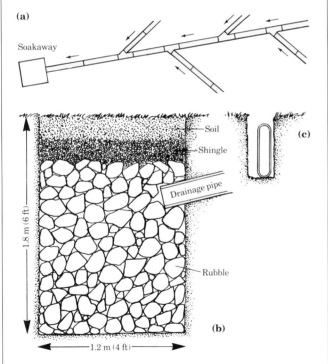

Fig. 6 It may be necessary to install a drainage system in a lawn site if the soil is very badly drained. Pipes are laid in a herring-bone formation (a), the main pipe leading to a soakaway (b). Some modern plastic land-drainage pipes are very narrow and can be laid in slit trenches (c).

achieved by using a straight-edge board and spirit level.

Now move the soil around the site, adding or taking it away as required, until the ground is level either with the tops of the pegs, or with predetermined marks on the pegs.

Make sure you do not mix subsoil with topsoil. And remember that you must maintain an even depth of topsoil.

Draining

Grass will not grow well in very wet conditions so if the site is inclined to lie wet or waterlogged after heavy rain you should consider taking steps to improve drainage. Very often deep digging, known as double digging, will have the desired effect, but if the problem is very severe you should consider installing a drainage system (Fig 6). This is best done after site levelling.

Installing a drainage system is somewhat easier today than it used to be (traditionally bulky clay land-drain pipes were used) for there are available narrow plastic land-drainage pipes which are laid in slit-like trenches.

A drainage system consists of one main drain with laterals leading into it and spaced 4.5 m (15 ft) apart – known as the herring-bone system. The main drain should slope to a soakaway at the lowest part of the garden and the laterals should slope to the main one. You will need to dig a soakaway at least 1.8 m (6 ft) deep and 1.2 m (4 ft) wide, and fill it with rubble.

Digging

The soil on a lawn site should be broken up deeply to ensure good penetration of the grass roots. Single digging (Fig. 7) should be adequate, unless the ground is very compacted or poorly drained, when double digging (Fig. 8) is recommended. It is certainly advisable for a new site.

Fig. 7 Single digging.

(a) Make a trench at one end of the site, the depth of the spade blade and 30 cm (12 in) wide.

Add bulky organic matter to the trench to improve soil texture.

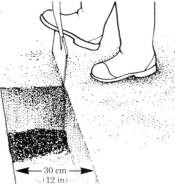

(b) Remove a second trench immediately behind it.

Throw the soil forward into the first one.

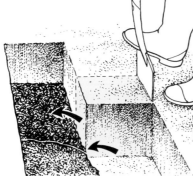

(c) Continue in this way, turning the spade upside down when throwing soil forward.

Add organic matter.

Continue in this way until the site has been dug.

Fig. 8 Double digging.

(a) Remove a trench 60 cm (2 ft) wide to depth of the spade blade.

Fork over the bottom to the depth of the fork's tines and then add bulky organic matter.

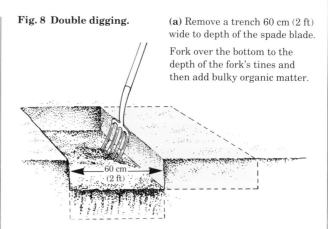

(b) Dig a second trench and throw the soil forward into the first, turning it over.

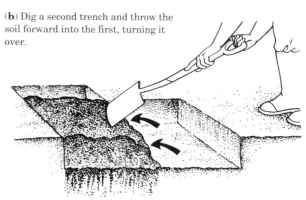

(c) Fork over the bottom, then add organic matter. Continue in this way.

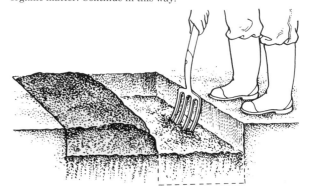

27

When digging you need to add various materials to each trench and to the topsoil to improve soil texture. Heavy and clayey soils can have grit or coarse sand added to improve drainage. All soils benefit from the addition of bulky organic matter, like sphagnum peat, composted bark or organic soil improver.

Firming the soil

Digging, of course, loosens the soil, and it must be given time to settle. That is why it is recommended that lawn-site preparation starts two to three months in advance of sowing or turfing.

Some weeks before you sow seed or lay turf, the dug soil must be firmed thoroughly. If it is not, it will sink eventually and give you an uneven lawn.

First you need to break down the roughly dug ground with a garden fork or metal rake. For a large site it would be more practical to use a rotary cultivator.

The most efficient way of firming the soil is by treading over the site with the weight on your heels. This must, of course, be done systematically to avoid leaving any 'soft spots'. Treading is both laborious and time consuming and is only practical on a small site. For large areas you will need to use a garden roller.

Now rake the soil level, remove any debris such as stones and carry out firming again.

Breaking down and firming must only be done when the soil is dry on the surface – never when wet or you will ruin the soil structure.

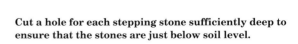

Stepping stones are generally laid on to well-firmed site.

Cut a hole for each stepping stone sufficiently deep to ensure that the stones are just below soil level.

Metal edging strip, to prevent damaged edges, is easy to install as it is simply inserted in a slit trench and the soil firmed really well on each side of it.

Paving and edgings

Once the soil has been firmed you can install stepping stones, paved areas for seats and ornaments, and edging materials.

● *Stepping stones* are generally laid onto well-firmed soil. Cut a hole in the ground for each one, firm the bottom and set the stone in place. Then firm the soil thoroughly all round. Set them 15–22 cm (6–9 in) apart and just below soil level.

● *Larger paved areas and paths alongside lawns* should have a firm foundation consisting of 10 cm (4 in) of hardcore over well-firmed soil and topped with 4 cm (1½ in) of soft builders' sand (Fig. 9a). Paving slabs are spot-bedded on mortar (1 part cement, 6 parts sand), five spots for each slab. Gently tap down each slab to ensure it is level (Fig. 9b). Laying slabs on 'blobs' of mortar will certainly save on your mortar bill, but this method does leave pockets under the slabs where ants, slugs, snails and all manner of creepy crawlies can breed with complete protection. For this reason, you might consider the alternative of laying the slabs on a level, thick bed of mortar. Leave 6 mm (¼ in) joints between slabs and grout them with mortar once their bedding mortar has set.

● *Paving bricks* are laid flat and not bedded on mortar. Leave 9 mm (³⁄₈ in) joints and fill with dry sand (Fig. 9c).

● *Metal or plastic edging strip* is simply inserted in a slit trench and the soil firmed really well on each site. It should be slightly below soil level.

Testing for pH

The degree of soil acidity or alkalinity is measured on the pH scale, which is numbered from 1 to 14 (the neutral point being 7.0) and can be ascertained by carrying out a simple soil test, say at the digging stage of site preparation. This is strongly advised,

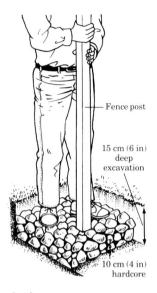

Fence post

15 cm (6 in) deep excavation

10 cm (4 in) hardcore

Fig 9. Paving a large area

◄(**a**) Paved areas and paths should have a firm foundation consisting of 10 cm (4 in) of hardcore over well-firmed soil. The hardcore can be compacted by ramming it down with a wooden fencing post. It is then covered with a layer of sand.

▼(**b**) Paving slabs are spot-bedded on mortar, five spots for each. Gently tap down each slab to ensure it is level and leave 6 mm (¼ in) joints between slabs which are later grouted with mortar.

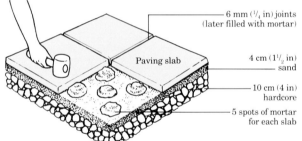

6 mm (¼ in) joints (later filled with mortar)

Paving slab

4 cm (1½ in) sand

10 cm (4 in) hardcore

5 spots of mortar for each slab

▼(**c**) Paving bricks for paths and other paved areas are laid flat on the layer of sand and not bedded on mortar. Tap them down to ensure they are level and later fill the joints with dry sand.

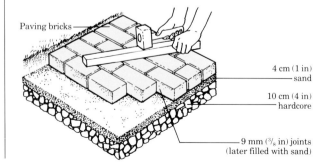

Paving bricks

4 cm (1 in) sand

10 cm (4 in) hardcore

9 mm (³⁄₈ in) joints (later filled with sand)

for if the soil is very acid (low pH) or very alkaline (high pH) a lawn may not make optimum growth. It is difficult to correct pH once a lawn has been created.

A simple soil-test kit can be obtained from a garden centre and should be used according to the accompanying instructions (Fig. 10). The optimum pH for lawns is between pH6 and 6.5, or slightly acid.

Apply ground limestone after digging if the soil is too acid, or dig in plenty of acidic peat if the soil is very alkaline. The instructions that come with soil-test kits generally advise how much lime to apply according to the pH, but if you are in any doubt then apply about 450 g per sq m (1 lb per sq yd).

Final preparations

Earlier on in this chapter the firming of the roughly dug lawn site was discussed, which also involved raking the soil level and removing any debris such as stones, sticks and the like. Now we come to final preparation of the site, just before sowing grass seed or laying turf.

After the above treatment, the soil should be uniformly firm all over and have a fine tilth, free from large lumps of soil and debris. At this stage, and about seven to ten days before sowing or turfing, a base dressing of fertilizer should be given, to get the newly germinated grass seedlings off to a good start.

It is advisable to use a fertilizer specially formulated for lawn-site preparation as then you know it has the right balance of nutrients or plant foods. For instance, one with an analysis of 10:15:10 of the major nutrients nitrogen, phosphorus and potassium.

This fertilizer should be applied according to the manufacturer's instructions, at the rate of 35 g per sq m (1 oz per sq yd). It can be applied by hand, but then there is the possibility that it may not be

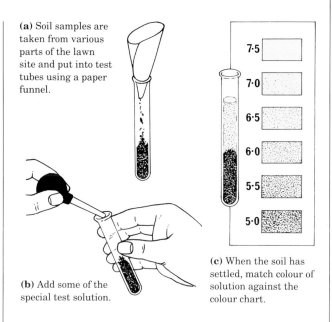

(a) Soil samples are taken from various parts of the lawn site and put into test tubes using a paper funnel.

(b) Add some of the special test solution.

(c) When the soil has settled, match colour of solution against the colour chart.

Fig. 10 **The degree of soil acidity or alkalinity, known as the pH, should be ascertained by carrying out a simple soil test with a proprietary kit.**

distributed evenly over the site or at the correct application rate. Far better would be to use a granular-fertilizer spreader. It comes with instructions on use and, of course, will be invaluable in the future, too, for applying lawn fertilizers, mosskillers and the like.

The fertilizer should be applied when the surface of the soil is dry but moist underneath and thoroughly raked into the soil surface with an iron garden rake.

Just before sowing or laying turf it is advisable to give the lawn site a final light raking, again using an iron garden rake, and again when the surface of the soil is dry. This will ensure a really fine tilth and give you a final opportunity of removing any remaining stones or debris and ensuring a really level surface.

This is how your lawn site should look after it has been prepared for sowing. It has been marked out into squares to make hand sowing of seed easier.

Hand sowing of grass seed is practical only for small lawn sites, as the care required to ensure thin and even sowing makes it quite a slow process.

LAWNS FROM SEED

When buying grass seed, one normally obtains a mixture of different kinds of grasses according to the quality of lawn one wants to create and suited to the soil type.

Fine ornamental

The fine ornamental lawn consists of fine-leaved grasses. This will not take a lot of hard wear and is really intended for setting off flower beds and borders. It requires a great deal of care and attention to keep it looking good, including frequent mowing.

Grass-seed mixture for fine lawns contain bent grasses (*Agrostis*) which have a creeping habit, and fescue grasses (*Festuca*), which may also be creeping or have a tufted habit of growth. Widely used in fine grass-seed mixtures is browntop bent (*Agrostis tenuis*) which is tolerant of dry and acid soils. It has good drought resistance.

The other major grass in fine seed mixtures is Chewing's fescue (*Festuca rubra commutata*) which also tolerates dry and acid soils, as well as alkaline conditions, and has good drought resistance. It is not suitable for clay soils. The habit is tufted.

Creeping red fescue (*Festuca rubra rubra*) is also often used and has a creeping habit. Best on light soils, it has good drought resistance. Not so suitable for clay soils.

Hardwearing utility

The hardwearing utility lawn is intended for heavy use, including games and general outdoor living. You need to choose a grass-seed mixture which contains tough, hardwearing grasses. These generally have broader leaves than bents and fescues and therefore create a lawn with a coarser texture. However, today there is available some finer-leaved kinds of perennial rye grass, one of the 'staples' of hardwearing utility mixtures.

The utility lawn needs less attention than the fine ornamental lawn and less mowing, so is ideal for the busy 'weekend' gardener.

The major grass of utility mixtures is perennial rye grass (*Lolium perenne*), or rather finer-leaved cultivars of it. Of tufted habit, it is suitable for all types of soil, including clay. It prefers a fertile moisture-retentive type.

Also often included in utility mixes are: crested dog's-tail (*Cynosurus cristatus*), tufted habit, suitable for all types of soil including clay, drought resistant; smooth-stalked meadow grass (*Poa pratensis*), creeping habit, tolerates sandy acid soils, good drought resistance; and rough-stalked meadow grass (*Poa trivialis*), which has a tufted habit, poor drought resistance, ideal for moist heavy soils.

There are a few grass-seed mixtures that are offered as 'easy maintenance'. With these the grass grows less rapidly, requiring less cutting.

Shade

Special mixtures are available for light shade. These might include the wood meadow grass (*Poa nemoralis*), a tufted grass that will not tolerate close mowing or drought; rough-stalked meadow grass (*Poa trivialis*); creeping red fescue (*Festuca rubra rubra*); and fine-leaved fescue (*Festuca tenuifolia*), suitable for dry soils.

Sowing grass seed

There are two recommended periods in the year for sowing grass seed: spring and early autumn. At these times the soil is warm – in spring it is warming up and in early autumn it still retains some warmth from the summer sun. Generally at these times, too, the soil is moist. These are the optimum conditions for the germination of grass

33

· A SELECTION OF GRASS-SEED MIXTURES ·

When buying a mixture, make sure it is suited to the purpose required and to the type of soil. The following are a few typical examples of seed mixtures one can expect to find. Parts by volume.

Mixture for a fine ornamental lawn
Browntop bent – two parts
Chewing's fescue – eight parts
Adaptable regarding soils but suitable for
dry and acid conditions

Chewings
fescue

Utility mixture for moist or clay soils
Perennial ryegrass – three parts
Rough-stalked meadow grass – two parts
Timothy – one part
Browntop bent – one part
Chewing's fescue – three parts

Perennial
ryegrass

Utility mixture for light and dry soils
Smooth-stalked meadow grass – four parts
Browntop bent – one part
Chewing's fescue – three parts
Creeping red fescue – two parts

Creeping red
fescue

Mixture for a shady site
Wood meadow grass – three parts
Rough-stalked meadow grass – five parts
Creeping red fescue – two parts

---

seed, and seedlings should appear within 10 days of sowing.

Within these periods sow only when conditions are suitable. For instance, the weather must be calm. The surface of the soil should be dry so that it will not stick to your shoes, but moist just underneath.

Just before sowing grass seed the lawn site should be lightly raked in one direction with an iron garden rake. This will result in mini furrows (rather like a ploughed field in miniature).

The amount of seed to sow on a given site needs working out carefully. Many people are surprised at how little grass seed is needed: it is sown at a rate of 35–70 g per sq m (1–2 oz per sq yd). Ideally aim for 50 g per sq m ($1^{1}/_{2}$ oz per sq yd).

● *Sowing techniques* For small areas sow by hand. The seed should be split into two equal portions. One portion is sown down the length of the site, and the second portion is sown across it. This helps to ensure even distribution. For real precision sowing, mark out the site into square metres (square yards) with strings and sow each one with the appropriate amount of seed (Fig. 11).

Hand sowing may not be practical for large areas, where a seed drill is recommended. It is probably not worth buying one of these so hire one for a day or weekend. Make sure it can be calibrated to apply the right quantity of seeds. Carry out a test run first, say on a garden path or area of concrete. Again, sow half the quantity of seed down the length of the site, and the other half across it.

After sowing, all you need do to cover the seeds with soil is to rake lightly across the mini-furrows to fill them in.

● *Aftercare* After sowing, pray for gentle rain! If this does not occur after several days water the site gently with a garden sprinkler.

Fig. 11 Sowing seed by hand

(a) Lightly rake the soil in one direction.

(b) For precision sowing, mark out site into square metres (yards) with string and sow at rate of 50g per sq m (1½ oz per sq yd).

● Sow half the amount down length of site, and the second half across it.

(c) Cover the seeds with soil by lightly raking in the opposite direction.

To prevent disturbance from birds, either tightly stretch black thread 8–10 cm (3–4 in) above the soil (Fig. 27 on p. 74), or lay brushwood over the surface.

Germinating grass seeds lightly lift the soil surface, so when the seedlings are 5–8 cm (2–3 in) high, lightly roll with a garden roller when the soil is dry.

The first mowing should take place when the grass is about 8 cm (3 in) high, using a really sharp mower to remove only 2.5 cm (1 in) of growth. (Height of cut is therefore 5 cm (2 in). Thereafter mow regularly, but no closer than 12 mm (½ in) during the first year.

LAWNS FROM TURF

Always buy turf from a specialist supplier as then it should be possible to choose a suitable type for soil and use and it will have been produced from proper lawn grasses. Also, it should be free from weeds (including coarse weed grasses) and supplied to a uniform thickness.

Traditionally turf is grown in fields by the suppliers. It may be grown from seed or it may be natural turf that has been established for years. Field-grown turf is still popular today. Normally it is supplied in 90 cm by 30 cm (3 ft by 1 ft) pieces, each one rolled for ease of delivery and handling. The pieces should be of uniform thickness.

There may be a very limited choice of grasses with traditional field-grown turf, with perhaps no choice for different soil types. The supplier may simply offer turves for utility and fine ornamental lawns. These turves have soil attached to the roots and are often quite heavy, depending on the thickness of the soil.

More modern is seedling turf which, as the name suggests, is raised from seed. This is still usually grown in fields, but one has a wide choice of grasses for different purposes and soils. Also, the special growing technique gives a very fibrous root system, so the turf can be lifted with virtually no soil attached. It is therefore very light in weight and is supplied in comparatively large rolls.

Laying turf
Traditional field-grown turf is best laid in autumn, winter or early spring as there is little risk of the soil drying out. Seedling turf should not be laid in winter. Never lay any turf in summer.

The site must be completely ready by the time the turves are delivered as they cannot be stored for long. Try to lay them immediately, although they can be left rolled up for two or three days, and they can be kept for a week or so by unrolling them on a spare piece of ground.

Start laying the turves, whether they are the traditional size or modern lightweight rolls, on one side of the site. Start with one row of 90 by 30 cm (3 by 1 ft) turves or a roll of seedling turf. Each piece must butt up tightly to the previous piece.

When laying turves never stand on the prepared soil or it will be disturbed. Work forward, facing the soil, but stand on wide planks of wood placed on the turf that has been laid.

If laying traditional 90 by 30 cm (3 by 1 ft) turves, stagger them like bricks in a wall. Do this by using

half turves in every other row. Rolls of turf are laid in strips, as per instructions from the supplier.

The turf should be firmed when laying is completed, using a light garden roller. Any gaps in the joints should be filled by brushing fine soil into them.

In dry periods water the new lawn heavily and regularly to help it establish and to prevent the turves from shrinking.

Light mowing can start when the grass starts to grow. Seedling turf should first be cut after two or three weeks, but no closer than 2.5 cm (1 in) for the first six weeks. Thereafter mow as for established lawns.

When laying turf it is usual to start on one side of the site. The half-moon iron shown here is a useful tool for cutting turves, although an old knife could be used.

OTHER AREAS

Turfing and seeding banks

One should not attempt to establish grass on very steep banks, for not only will it be difficult, but subsequent maintenance will be even more so.

But gently sloping banks can certainly be grassed down. It is best to disturb the soil as little as possible: simply rake it to produce a surface tilth and incorporate a base fertilizer.

To prevent turves from slipping down the bank before they have rooted, hold them in place with short wooden pegs inserted through them and into the soil below.

Never stand on the prepared soil when laying, but on a plank of wood placed on the turf that has been laid. This prevents disturbance to the prepared soil.

Establishing a long-grass area

To create a wild-flower meadow you should start with a fallow site, prepared as described earlier for a normal lawn. Success will never be achieved by sowing wild flowers in an established lawn, and besides the grasses are totally unsuitable as they are too vigorous and would smother the flowers.

If you want to turn an existing lawn into a wild-flower meadow, the grass should first be killed off by spraying it with a weedkiller containing glyphosate, used according to the maker's instructions and while the weeds are in active growth.

Turves of traditional size are staggered like bricks in a wall. This is accomplished by using shorter turves in every other row. Firm the turf after laying.

• HANDY TIP •

When planting bulbs it is important to ensure that their bases are in close contact with the soil in the bottom of the holes. If they are suspended in the holes, with air space below them, they will not root into the soil and consequently will fail to grow. Invariably when bulbs do not grow the supplier is blamed, but all too often it is due to faulty planting.

As with sowing ordinary grass seed, a fine tilth will be needed. The best sowing time for a grass seed and wild-flower mixture is early autumn. Alternatively sowing can be undertaken between early and mid-spring.

Thin sowing is absolutely essential, the recommended rate being 25 g per sq m ($^3/_4$ oz per sq yd). Thick sowing results in too many grasses in the area and these will then compete with the wild flowers and probably smother them out.

Creating fragrant lawns

Chamomile, thyme and mint lawns are best created in the spring, when the soil is warming up and drying out, as then the plants will rapidly become established. Planted in cold wet soil they may rot off before they have a chance to establish.

Try to find a nursery supplying these plants as a fair quantity will be needed, even to create a small lawn. It is very unlikely that sufficient plants will be available from the average garden centre. Young pot-grown plants are best.

The site will need to be prepared as for an ordinary lawn and it is absolutely essential that it is completely free from perennial weeds as these will be impossible to eradicate once the lawn has been planted.

Before planting, water the plants thoroughly to ensure the compost is moist right the way through. If the plants have a dry rootball when they are planted they may not establish and may even die, because it is often impossible to moisten it after planting, no matter how much water is subsequently applied. Plant them with a trowel, 15 cm (6 in) apart each way, firming the soil moderately around the rootball.

Planting bulbs in grass

Spring-flowering bulbs to be grown in lawns are planted in early to mid-autumn, in bold irregular drifts, say around and under specimen trees, in the corners or along the edges.

The ideal situation would be to plant the bulbs before grass seed is sown or turves laid, but this is not always possible. However, it is certainly a practical proposition to plant bulbs in an established lawn, and this is probably what most gardeners do.

There are two ways of planting bulbs in established turf. If you have quite large quantities to plant it would be best to lift the turf wherever drifts of bulbs are required, plant the bulbs, then replace the turf (Fig. 5 on p. 19). It is laid as described earlier in this chapter and should be watered until re-established if conditions are dry.

Bulbs can be planted with a hand trowel or with a bulb planter which takes out a core of soil, this being replaced when the bulb has been placed in the hole.

Bulbs should not be planted uniformly but at random to make the drifts look more natural. To achieve this, simply scatter handfuls of bulbs over the ground and plant them where they have fallen.

The small or dwarf bulbs recommended in the previous chapter are planted 8 cm (3 in) deep – that is, they have this depth of soil over them – and 8 cm apart each way.

·3·

Keeping up Appearances

It is no good hiding the fact that a lawn is one of the most labour-intensive parts of the garden. If you want a high-quality, dense sward of grass you have to lavish quite a bit of care on it throughout the year. Remember that a badly maintained lawn will be an eye-sore in the garden.

Of course, not all grass areas are labour intensive. A wild-flower meadow, in which the grass is allowed to grow long, is the most labour saving, as it needs cutting only twice a year, in summer and autumn. Even more labour-saving are non-grass lawns consisting of chamomile, thymes or creeping mints.

So what does a lawn need to keep it looking good all year round? Mowing is one of the most frequent jobs and is carried out for much of the year. The frequency will depend on the type of lawn you have – a fine ornamental lawn will need more mowing than a utility one.

For this task to be easy and efficient you will need the right type of mower for the job and it should be well maintained, with the blades razor sharp.

The lawn edges should be well maintained and regularly trimmed. If allowed to grow long or become broken they will ruin the overall appearance of the lawn.

There are several mundane but essential tasks that need to be carried out each year. Feeding is very important to maintain dense healthy growth. You will also need to remove dead grass and other debris and this is achieved by scarifying and raking. Aerating helps to get air to the roots which ensures healthy growth, and the icing on the cake is topdressing, whereby you work a special compost into the lawn surface to keep the soil in good condition and ensure a 'springy' feel to the lawn.

If there are no restrictions on garden watering then it is certainly worthwhile watering the lawn regularly in dry periods or drought to prevent the grass from turning brown.

All of these jobs and techniques are described in detail in this chapter, plus the equipment and tools you will need to carry them out.

MOWERS AND MOWING

As mowing is the most frequent job that needs to be carried out on lawns, and requires to be done efficiently, it is worthwhile buying the best-quality mower you can afford, making sure it is suited to the job and keeping it well maintained.

Choosing a mower

There is a wide range of mowers to choose from, both hand-propelled and self-propelled. The latter are powered by petrol engines or electric motors. With electricity one has the choice of mains or battery. Self-propelled mowers are almost essential for large lawns, the hand machines being suited only to small areas. Mains-electric mowers may not be suitable for large lawns, either, due to the long length of electric cable that would be needed.

● *Petrol-driven mowers* are noisier, need more maintenance than electric mowers and are more expensive to run. They have more power, though, than electric models.

● *Mains-electric mowers* should always be used in conjunction with a residual current device which is simply plugged into the socket and which cuts off the electricity supply in a 'micro-second' should you damage the cable or something goes wrong with the machine, so saving you from electrocution.

● *Battery-operated mowers* are another alternative but the batteries will need charging up frequently.

Basically there are two types of lawnmower – cylinder and rotary. With the former, the blades, which vary in number, are in the form of a cylinder which revolves horizontally against a fixed blade. With rotary mowers the blades (generally two) rotate at high speed and cut the grass by slashing it – rather like a scythe.

● *Cylinder mowers* Fine ornamental lawns are generally cut with cylinder mowers as they are capable of providing a fine, even cut. They can only be used on level surfaces and are no good for rough or long grass or uneven lawns.

Cylinder mowers may be hand- and self-propelled. Some hand machines have side wheels while others run on rollers. Rear-roller models give a striped effect. Cylinder mowers with five or six blades are recommended only for utility lawns, as they give a coarse cut. For fine ornamental lawns you need one with more blades – up to 10 or 12 – to give a fine cut. Cylinder mowers come in various cutting widths and generally have a grass box to collect the clippings.

Some powered cylinder mowers are self-propelled; others have to be pushed but the blades are powered, so giving a fine cut.

● *Rotary mowers* are particularly suitable for cutting rough or long grass. With hand-propelled ones only the blades are powered, so are suitable only for small areas of grass. They generally move on side wheels. Self-propelled models may run on wheels or rollers, the latter giving a striped effect. Many rotaries these days have grass boxes or bags for collecting the clippings as you mow.

● *Hover mowers* are rotaries but float on a cushion of air. They are very easy to use and are powered by electric motors or petrol engines. Some models have boxes or bags for collecting the clippings. Hovers are recommended only for utility lawns and rough-grass areas. Contrary to popular advice, they should never be used on steep banks.

Where to see and buy

Where can one go to see lawn mowers to compare the various makes and models, and where can one buy?

You might first of all check your local garden centres. Many of these have a garden machinery section, often operated by a separate company. Here, of course, you will be able to see a wide range of mowers and you will be able to obtain sound advice from the staff on what would be best for your purposes. There are also garden-machinery companies independent of garden centres.

One can also buy lawn mowers from DIY superstores and from various high-street chain stores. Understandably, the range is more limited and consists of the most popular mowers. You may not be able to obtain expert advice from these sources, but the main attraction is that the mowers are often cheaper than those offered by specialists.

A cylinder mower with rear roller is the best choice for a fine ornamental lawn as it provides a fine, even cut – and the all-important striped effect.

Maintenance of mowers

It cannot be stressed too strongly that regular maintenance and servicing of mowers is essential, for not only will they keep running but the blades will always be really sharp, which makes for efficient cutting. Blunt blades will simply pull and bruise the grass rather than cut it.

If you are not technically minded, have power and hand mowers serviced annually by a proper garden machinery company. They will carry out a full service and sharpen the blades, or replace badly worn or damaged ones.

Garden machinery companies, as mentioned in the previous section under 'Where to see and buy', are invariably able to carry out the servicing of lawn mowers, and indeed all other kinds of garden machinery. Some even have their own collection and delivery service, which is a boon to those without a car; but even if you have a car it is worth making use of such a service as it is sometimes difficult to get machinery like lawn mowers into it!

Fig. 12 Sharpening the blades of cylinder mowers.

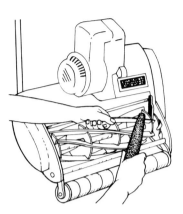

(**a**) Blades can be sharpened with a special sharpening tool or, shown here, with a carborundum stone, following the instructions in the manual.

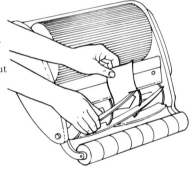

(**b**) Test for sharpness by getting the blades to cut a strip of paper. If it is cut cleanly, as opposed to being torn, then you know they are sharp and will cut the grass well.

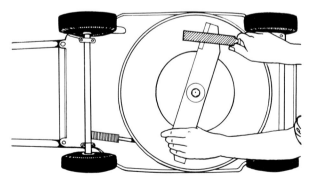

Fig. 13 Metal blades of rotary mowers can usually be sharpened with a file: again, though, do follow the advice on blade sharpening given in the manual.

Have the mower serviced in the winter so that it is ready for use in spring. Many gardeners do not think of having their mowers serviced until they are about to start using them again: consequently, garden machinery companies are often run off their feet in spring and it could, therefore, take several weeks to have a mower serviced.

If you want to carry out your own servicing follow instructions in the manual. There is much you can do yourself to keep your mower in good condition, even if you are not technically minded. The manual will give you full details. For instance, it is quite an easy matter to sharpen blades with a special sharpening tool or carborundum stone, or with a file (Figs. 12 and 13).

Each time you finish using the mower remove adhering grass and mud from the blades and any other parts, especially the underside. Use a stiff hand brush. Then wash clean, dry and rub bare metal surfaces with an oily rag to prevent rusting. This applies especially to cutting edges of blades and the undersides of rotary mowers. Any rusty areas can first be rubbed down with emery paper to remove the rust.

Carry out regular lubrication, again following instructions in the manual (Fig. 14). Do not forget to recharge a battery mower immediately after use, nor to top up the battery as necessary with distilled water. The oil level of petrol mowers should be checked weekly and topped up if necessary. Regularly check the cutting action of cylinder mowers and adjust if necessary. The distance between cylinder and fixed blade must be correct.

Mowing techniques

Lawns are mown during the spring, summer and autumn, when the grass is growing. Occasional mowing may be needed in winter if the grass is making some growth.

Always mow when the lawn is dry as the mower

may damage it or create muddy patches if very wet. Never mow if the grass is frozen as this can cause bruising – unsightly black marks.

A lawn should never be mown during a drought, when it is making little if any growth.

The best advice when it comes to frequency of mowing, is to mow regularly but not too closely. Fine ornamental lawns should be mown every two or three days, utility lawns ideally every three or five days, but they can be mown every seven days if you do not have much time.

Lawns in shade should be mown less frequently than those in sunny situations as the grasses used in mixtures for shade do not like close mowing. Never cut shady lawns hard – certainly no lower than about 2.5 cm (1 in).

The height at which a lawn is cut should vary with the seasons, and depends on the type of lawn. Let us first consider the fine ornamental lawn. During the spring and summer it should be cut to between 6 and 12 mm ($\frac{1}{4}$ and $\frac{1}{2}$ in). In autumn and early spring, plus winter if you need to mow during that season, the height of cut should be raised to 19 mm ($\frac{3}{4}$ in).

Utility lawns are cut to a height of 12–25 mm ($\frac{1}{2}$–1 in) during spring and summer. In the autumn and early spring (and again in winter if mowing is

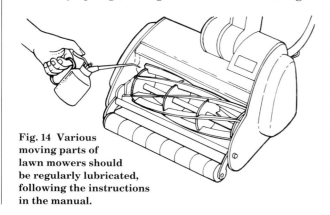

Fig. 14 Various moving parts of lawn mowers should be regularly lubricated, following the instructions in the manual.

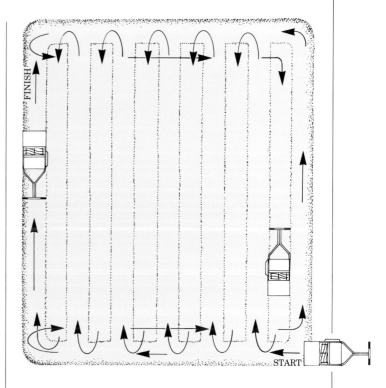

Fig. 15 Lawns should be mown systematically. If you want a striped effect, follow this sequence; first each end of the lawn should be cut by mowing across it. The main area is then cut by taking the mower up and down it. Each cut should slightly overlap the previous one.

needed) they should be cut less hard, to a height of 25–38 mm (1–1$\frac{1}{2}$ in).

Before you mow a lawn make sure it is free from debris such as stones, twigs, paper and so on. Never run a mower over wormcasts (those little heaps of soil produced by worms' activities) as it will flatten them, resulting in muddy patches which will smother the grass. They should be thoroughly scattered by brushing the lawn with a stiff broom – a besom made of birch or similar twigs is ideal for this purpose.

A lawn should be mown systematically to ensure

that every square centimetre is covered and to create a pleasing appearance. For instance, if you want a striped effect, which is most pronounced with a mower fitted with a rear roller, follow this sequence: first each end of the lawn should be cut by mowing across it, plus any awkward shaped areas. The main area is then cut by taking the mower systematically up and down it. Each cut should slightly overlap the previous one to ensure you do not leave any grass uncut (Fig. 15).

The direction of mowing should be changed each time as this has the effect of helping to control coarse weed grasses and may help to rectify any previous mowing faults.

Mowing is not so straightforward as many people imagine. A common fault is scalping the lawn – cutting off all the grass to expose the soil. This can occur if you run the mower over high or low spots in the lawn. These areas need correcting as described in Chapter 6 (see page 87).

● Mangled or torn grass is caused by blunt or incorrectly set mower blades, or a damaged fixed blade on cylinder mowers.
Cure: adjust, sharpen or repair the blades as necessary.

● If the grass is too long for the mower setting you are liable to get a ribbed effect when mowing – narrow strips of alternate long and short grass.
Cure: raise the height of cut.

● A corrugated effect is caused by always mowing in the same direction, especially with a powered mower.
Cure: change direction of cut each time.

◀ **Rotary mowers also give a good finish and are particularly suitable for rough or long grass areas.**

▶ **Hover mowers are recommended only for utility lawns and rough-grass areas. They are very easy to use.**

Look after yourself

Earlier in this chapter it was recommended that a residual current device is used in conjunction with a mains electric lawn mower (and indeed with other electrical equipment). But there are several other aspects of safety to bear in mind. For instance, wear stout leather boots or shoes when mowing and using an electric trimmer. Never wear loose flowing clothing and dangling scarves or pendants as they may get caught up in the machinery.

An electric cable should always be slung over one shoulder. If you need to attend to a mower or trimmer for any reason, stop the engine or motor first and, in the case of electric machinery, remove the plug from the socket.

What to do with the clippings

The general consensus of opinion is that grass clippings are best removed from the lawn. Therefore, if the lawnmower is fitted with a grass-collecting box or bag, then use it. If not, it is recommended that you rake up the clippings on completion of mowing.

However, it should be said that very fine clippings will not harm the lawn if left, provided there is only a light scattering, the result of frequent mowing. In fact, they will help to return nutrients and humus to the soil and assist in moisture conservation during dry conditions. A thick scattering of clippings, though, would smother the grass, lead to thatch (a matted layer of dead grass) and encourage worms and lawn diseases.

How can clippings be disposed of? The answer is they shouldn't, as they are among the finest ingredients of the compost heap. Make sure you mix them thoroughly with other materials before adding them to the heap. However, do not put the clippings from the first cut after an application of hormone lawn weedkiller onto the compost heap, but take them by bag to the local refuse tip.

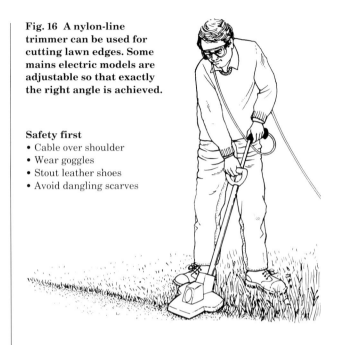

Fig. 16 A nylon-line trimmer can be used for cutting lawn edges. Some mains electric models are adjustable so that exactly the right angle is achieved.

Safety first
• Cable over shoulder
• Wear goggles
• Stout leather shoes
• Avoid dangling scarves

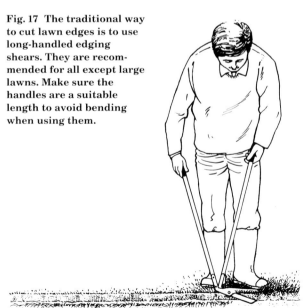

Fig. 17 The traditional way to cut lawn edges is to use long-handled edging shears. They are recommended for all except large lawns. Make sure the handles are a suitable length to avoid bending when using them.

LAWN EDGING AND TRIMMING

To keep the lawn looking neat and tidy the edges will need cutting regularly, together with any awkward places where the mower cannot reach such as around the base of mature trees where the grass grows right up to the trunks, around overhanging shrubs, and along walls and fences.

The nylon-line trimmer is one of the best pieces of garden equipment ever invented, for not only can it be used for cutting down weeds in various parts of the garden, but on the lawn it can be used for the above purposes. Some mains electric trimmers are adjustable so that exactly the right angle is achieved for cutting the edges. A trimmer can be used right up to the trunks of trees and other objects without damaging them (Fig. 16).

Most small-garden owners will opt for a mains electric trimmer, but for larger gardens one powered by a small petrol engine would be more practical and convenient.

Always wear goggles to protect your eyes when using a nylon-line trimmer.

There are other ways of cutting the lawn edges, of course. The traditional way is to use long-handled edging shears. These are recommended for all except large lawns. Make sure you buy a model with a suitable length of handle, to avoid bending when using them. Always keep the blades razor sharp to ensure a clean cut (Fig. 17).

Another alternative is the roller lawn edger whereby a disc blade rotates against a fixed blade as the tool is pushed along the lawn edge. Do try it out if possible before you buy, as you may not find it as easy to use or as efficient as edging shears.

Yet another choice is the electric (mains or battery) lawn edger, ideal for large lawns.

Apart from nylon-line trimmers mentioned above, what other pieces of equipment are there for cutting awkward areas, around tree trunks, and the like? For small lawns there are long-handled lawn shears. As with edging shears, try to make sure the handles are of a suitable length for you.

Ordinary garden shears can be used for all of the above tasks, but this means kneeling down and so these are only practical with the tiniest of lawns.

OTHER REGULAR TASKS

There are numerous other tasks that need to be carried out regularly but not as frequently as mowing, edging and trimming, to maintain the lawn in peak condition. Mowing alone is insufficient as in the end you will have a thin patchy lawn dominated by moss and weeds.

Scarifying

This is basically very vigorous raking of the lawn to remove dead grass, which is known as thatch. Dead grass builds up into a layer between the leaves of the grass and the surface of the soil. Simply left, it will form a thick dense layer which will prevent moisture from penetrating the soil. Only long periods of rain or artificial watering will ensure moisture gets through thick thatch.

· WHEN AND WHEN NOT TO SCARIFY ·	
Early autumn	This is the period for scarifying to remove thatch. Also it will encourage the grass to produce side shoots. The raking should be deep. Make sure any moss present has first been killed
Spring	Never scarify during most of this season as the spaces it produces will not be filled with side shoots
Late spring and summer	Scarify in moderation only to remove moss that has been killed with a mosskiller. Only rake the moss patches – not the entire lawn

But it is not only moisture that may fail to get through thatch. Air will be prevented from reaching the roots of the grass, together with fertilizers. Thatch can also result in the lawn becoming less resistant to drought, a build-up of lawn diseases, and pools of water lying on the surface after rain or irrigation.

So how do you scarify a lawn? The traditional way is the hard way – raking vigorously with a spring-tine lawn rake (it has flexible steel tines). Rake in various directions to remove the thatch,

working methodically over the lawn. This method is only practical for small lawns.

Much easier, and certainly recommended for large lawns, is the motorized scarifier, which looks like an electric lawnmower. Use it first down the length of the lawn, then across it.

Raking

Raking is carried out at various times of the year as and when required to remove debris on the surface of the lawn. As with scarification, you can again use

◄ Scarifying, by raking vigorously with a spring-tine lawn rake. This autumn operation removes dead grass, known as thatch, and so helps the lawn to 'breathe'.

► An electric scarifier, ideal for removing dead grass from large lawns. You will be absolutely amazed how much dead material this machine removes.

a wire-tine lawn rake with flexible tines. There is another rake that you can use on lawns – the split-cane rake. As the name suggests, the tines are formed of flexible cane.

Raking is a more gentle operation than scarification – one is not aiming to remove rubbish right down to soil level. An important time for raking is in autumn, to remove leaves that have fallen from deciduous trees and shrubs.

Early spring is another major time for raking, to clear up any rubbish that has accumulated over winter, such as twigs and any remaining leaves.

Raking can be carried out after application of mosskillers to remove dead moss. In this case slightly more vigorous raking will be needed.

Raking occasionally in spring and summer is worthwhile if there are creeping weeds in the lawn as it helps in their control by raising them up and exposing them to the lawn mower.

Aerating

This consists of making a series of holes or slits all over the lawn to cure soil compaction caused by heavy use and by mowing (Fig. 18).

Deep aeration, to a depth of 10–15 cm (4–6 in), to cure deep soil compaction, is carried out in early autumn. On small lawns a garden fork can be used. Push it in vertically then gently ease it backwards and forwards. Insert it at intervals of 10–15 cm (4–6 in) all over the lawn.

For heavy or waterlogged soils carry out deep aeration every three years with a hollow-tine aerator which removes cores of soil. Insert the tool at 10–15 cm (4–6 in) intervals. Follow with topdressing to improve condition of the soil.

Fig. 18 Aeration for compacted soil. The idea is to create holes and slits which will allow the soil to 'breathe' and water to penetrate.

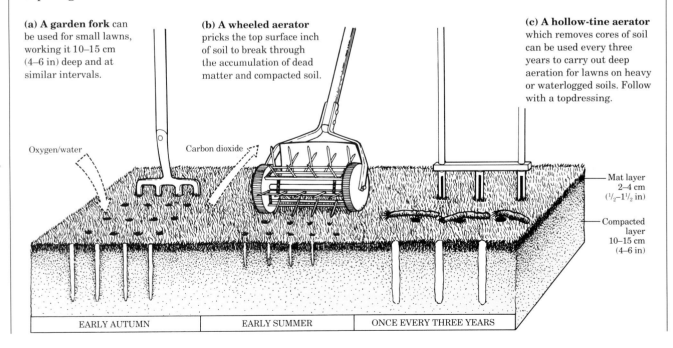

(a) A garden fork can be used for small lawns, working it 10–15 cm (4–6 in) deep and at similar intervals.

(b) A wheeled aerator pricks the top surface inch of soil to break through the accumulation of dead matter and compacted soil.

(c) A hollow-tine aerator which removes cores of soil can be used every three years to carry out deep aeration for lawns on heavy or waterlogged soils. Follow with a topdressing.

Oxygen/water

Carbon dioxide

Mat layer 2–4 cm ($\frac{1}{2}$–1$\frac{1}{2}$ in)

Compacted layer 10–15 cm (4–6 in)

EARLY AUTUMN | EARLY SUMMER | ONCE EVERY THREE YEARS

Fig. 19 A general-purpose topdressing mixture is easily made up at home with ingredients bought from a garden centre.

1 part peat + 3 parts loam + 6 parts sand

Light surface aeration, such as making slits in the lawn, is carried out in spring and summer if necessary.

Aerating large lawns is best carried out with an aerating machine, powered or hand-propelled. Generally the tines can be changed to suit the job – they may be solid, hollow or blade-like, the latter making slits.

Topdressing

This involves applying a mixture of loam, sand and peat to the lawn in early autumn to improve the soil. Also it helps to create a more level surface. Unless the soil is very poor, there is no need for topdressing every year. If aeration is planned too, carry it out before topdressing.

You can make up your own mixture (Fig. 19) or buy a proprietary topdressing. A good general-purpose mix is three parts loam, one part peat and six parts sand (parts by bulk). This can be modified to suit the soil – more sand for heavy or clay soil, less sand and perhaps more peat for sandy conditions.

Spread the mixture evenly with a shovel. The average rate of application is 1.8 kg per sq m (4 lb per sq yd), but this can be increased to 3 kg per sq m (7 lb per sq yd) if the surface is very uneven. Work it well down to the soil surface with the back of a rake or with a purpose-made tool, known as a lute (Fig. 20).

Never allow topdressing to lie on the surface – if you cannot work it all in, remove the excess.

Fig. 20 Topdressing mix should be worked well down to the soil surface. The back of a rake can be used or, as shown here, a purpose-made tool known as a lute.

Top dressing

◄ Spreading lawn fertilizer by hand, whether to a prepared site as here or to an established lawn, is made easier by first marking out the area with string into 1m³ (3 ft) squares.

▶ Granular lawn fertilizers can be applied very evenly and at the correct rate by using a fertilizer distributor. Most lawn-fertilizer manufacturers offer them.

Feeding

Feeding is one of the most important aspects of lawn care as it replaces the nutrients that are so quickly used up by the grass.

Use proper lawn fertilizers, which contain the three major nutrients: nitrogen to promote leaf growth, phosphorus to ensure healthy root growth, and potassium which hardens growth, making it more tolerant of cold conditions and drought. Some lawn fertilizers also contain weedkillers and/or mosskillers, so enabling you to 'feed and weed' in one operation.

There are two main periods in the year when feeding should be carried out. Firstly, spring, using

The other main period for fertilizer application is autumn. Sadly, so many people neglect autumn feeding, yet it is very important as it prepares the grass for the ravages of winter. Autumn lawn fertilizers (which may also contain the mosskiller ferrous sulphate), contain a relatively large amount of potash and are low in nitrogen. Use during a mild spell in early autumn.

Fertilizers must be applied strictly according to instructions on the containers or damage could result. The grass should be dry during application, but the soil below moist. Never feed during a drought. Water in granular fertilizer if there is no rain within two days.

Fertilizer must be applied evenly and at the correct rate. It is best to use a fertilizer distributor for granular fertilizers (you can buy one at any garden centre). Set it to the correct application rate as recommended by the manufacturer, then apply the fertilizer in parallel strips, but avoid overlapping.

Liquid fertilizers can be applied with a watering can fitted either with a rose or, for more even application, a dribble bar. Alternatively use a hose end feeder which automatically mixes plant food with water, enabling you to feed and water the lawn at the same time. Use an appropriate soluble spring and summer lawn fertilizer.

Watering
Watering is highly recommended during dry spells to prevent the grass from turning brown. Although it will recover, 'browning off' will weaken it and then weeds and moss may invade. Unfortunately, it may not be possible to carry out garden watering in some areas as there may be a ban on it during the summer because of water shortage. However, many of the aspects of lawn care discussed earlier will help to make lawns more resistant to dry periods or drought.

a fertilizer intended for spring and summer use containing a relatively large amount of nitrogen.

Additional feeding can be carried out in summer, especially if you feel the lawn needs a boost. Use a fertilizer formulated for spring and summer use. Liquid feeds, which give a quick boost to growth, are often used during this season.

Try to commence watering before the lawn starts to turn brown. If there has been no rain in the spring or summer for a week or ten days then that is the time to start artificial watering.

Once you start watering you should continue until the rain starts again. The frequency depends on soil type. Light free-draining sandy soils will need watering more often than heavy or clay soils, which are able to hold onto moisture for longer. On average, though, think in terms of watering once a week.

If the soil is hard and very dry on the surface then shallow spike or slit it before watering (see 'Aerating' on p. 50). This will help water to penetrate.

How much water should be applied each time? About 18 litres per sq m (4 gal per sq yd) each week is about right. This equals about 2.5 cm (1 in) of rain. Even better, if you can manage it, would be to apply this amount of water in two sessions, three days apart, as optimum penetration through the soil should then be achieved. The amount can be measured by standing empty tins over the part of the lawn being watered. When these have 2.5 cm (1 in) of water in them, you know you have applied enough.

To apply this amount of water you will need a garden sprinkler. There are various types available, from those with no moving parts, ideal for tiny lawns, to rotary and oscillating sprinklers for larger lawns.

Remember, when using a hosepipe connected to the mains water supply, it is now a legal requirement to install a back-siphonage protection device to prevent water supplies from being contaminated.

Looking after other areas

Finally, let us look at the maintenance requirements of banks, long-grass areas for wild flowers, areas where bulbs are growing and non-grass lawns.

● *Banks* Of course, to keep the grass short, you will need to carry out regular cutting as for normal lawns. However, never use a mower (not even a hover mower) on a steep bank as this is dangerous practice. Instead cut the grass with a nylon-line trimmer. Other lawn treatments also apply to banks, provided you can manage them.

● *The long-grass area* (or wild-flower meadow) should be mown in mid-summer, when the wild flowers will be over, and again in early autumn. The height of cut should be 5 cm (2 in) and the hay must be raked off. A wild-flower meadow needs little feeding.

● *Bulbs* Wherever these are planted in lawns, the grass should not be cut until their foliage has completely died down. Premature removal of the bulbs' leaves will lead to a poor flower display the following year.

● *Non-grass lawns* need very little attention. Chamomile should be given a light trim with shears or mower in late summer to keep it looking neat. Thymes and mints can be trimmed lightly after flowering to remove dead blooms and to maintain a neat habit of growth. Feed once a year in spring with a general-purpose fertilizer such as Growmore, but make sure it does not lodge on the foliage.

·4·
Weeding out Intruders

This chapter is about weeds. They are found everywhere in gardens, including lawns, and their control accounts for a large proportion of routine maintenance.

Thorough preparation of the site for a new lawn will have eradicated perennial weeds. However, soon after sowing grass seed, a crop of weed seedlings will appear with the grasses. There is no need to worry about these as they will soon die out when mowing starts.

With really good lawn care weeds will give minimal trouble as the grass will be so dense that they will have difficulty in becoming established. Some perennial weeds that are found in gardens cannot establish in lawns, anyway, for they will not tolerate frequent mowing. These include such normally pernicious kinds as ground elder (*Aegopodium podagraria*), stinging nettle (*Urtica dioica*), field bindweed (*Convolvulus arvensis*) and couch grass (*Agropyron repens*), which can be a real problem in beds and borders.

Annual weeds are even less trouble in lawns than perennial kinds. Again, they are more of a problem in beds and borders. Regular mowing eradicates most of them.

Frequent visitors

The types of weeds that are able to establish in and colonize lawns are perennials of low-growing habit and are therefore untouched by the mower. Some of these 'lawns weeds' have a mat-forming habit of growth, such as white clover (*Trifolium repens*) and yarrow (*Achillea millefolium*). Others have a rosette-forming habit, like dandelion (*Taraxacum officinale*) and plantain (*Plantago* species).

There are certain weed grasses which can establish in lawns, mainly perennial but also one or two annuals. These have coarse leaves and can form unsightly patches in lawns. They are difficult to control, as lawn weedkillers will not eradicate them, these being effective only on the broad-leaved weeds mentioned above.

Moss is a big problem for many lawn owners. These primitive plants very quickly colonize thin turf, but again will have difficulty in establishing in dense well-cared-for lawns. Moss is easily killed with mosskillers.

Algae or slime, and lichens are other primitive plants that may invade lawns. Again, though, they are easily controlled.

BROAD-LEAVED WEEDS

Here we look at the most common broad-leaved weeds of lawns. The broad-leaved kinds are the mat- and rosette-formers which hold their leaves horizontally, and therefore have the effect of smothering lawn grasses.

Bird's-foot trefoil (*Lotus corniculatus*)
This is a common lawn weed of alkaline or chalky soils. It is not unattractive, but should not be encouraged in lawns. It has slender creeping stems bearing trifoliate leaves and can quickly form large patches. The yellow pea-like flowers are carried in clusters. Surprisingly for a slender plant, it produces a deep taproot so it is able to resist drought.
● It generally takes two applications of lawn weedkiller to eradicate this weed.

Black medick (*Medicago lupulina*)
This is not one of the most serious weeds of lawns but it can be a problem in some situations, especially in areas with dry soil, where it will quickly invade thin lawns. It is somewhat like a clover, with trifoliate leaves and creeping stems, but it has heads of yellow flowers.
● This annual weed can be controlled by two applications of lawn weedkiller.

Bulbous buttercup (*Ranunculus bulbosus*)
Despite its pretty yellow flowers this is an unwelcome visitor. It has lobed and toothed leaves and a bulb-like basal stem. It is often found on alkaline and light sandy soils.
● One or two applications of lawn weedkiller will eradicate it.

◄ The daisy, *Bellis perennis*, is a very common lawn weed and it grows anywhere. The white flowers are attractive!

► If a lawn is neglected it will soon become full of weeds such as daisies, dandelions and speedwell.

Cat's-ear (*Hypochaeris radicata*)
Produces yellow daisy- or dandelion-like flowers on erect stalks, and carries its long wavy-edged leaves in a rosette. Grows in any soil.
● One or two applications of lawn weedkiller will control it. Suitable for spot treatment.

Creeping buttercup (*Ranunculus repens*)
Similar to bulbous buttercup but has a vigorous creeping habit and is common on wet or heavy soil.
● Killed with one application of lawn weedkiller.

· THE WORST BROAD-LEAVED WEEDS ·

Name	Description	Control
Daisy (*Bellis perennis*)	Very common, vigorous mat-former; smothers grasses; grows anywhere; white daisy flowers	One or two applications of lawn weedkiller
Pearlwort (*Sagina procumbens*)	Creeping mat-former that can smother grasses; grows anywhere; minute leaves and flowers; soon reappears after treatment with weedkiller if turf is thin	One application of lawn weedkiller is usually sufficient
White clover (*Trifolium repens*)	Rampant mat-forming weed capable of colonizing large areas; trifoliate leaves, white flowers, stem rooting; continues growing in drought	Rake lawn before mowing; one dose of weedkiller
Woodrush (*Luzula sylvestris*)	A problem on acid, sandy soil; difficult to control; grassy, hairy leaves, heads of brown flowers	Several applications of weedkiller needed
Yarrow (*Achillea millefolium*)	Spreads by creeping stems; mat former that is difficult to control; drought resistant; feathery foliage, flat heads of white flowers	Rake before mowing; several applications of weedkiller needed

Crowfoot (*Ranunculus acris*)
This is also known as the meadow buttercup. It is a common lawn weed but not so widespread as its cousin the creeping buttercup. It favours soils that are moisture retentive. It looks rather like the bulbous buttercup, but without the swollen stem base, having deeply toothed, lobed leaves and yellow buttercup flowers on tall upright stems. It has a tufted habit of growth.
● Generally two applications of lawn weedkiller are needed to kill this buttercup. Single plants can be removed by hand or spot treated with weedkiller.

Dandelion (*Taraxacum officinale*)
Produces a large rosette of long jagged-edged leaves and yellow daisy flowers on tall, thick, erect stems. Has a single, long, thick taproot. Grows anywhere.
● Remove by hand (including root). One or two applications of lawn weedkiller (spot treatment for single plants).

Lesser celandine (*Ranunculus ficaria*)
Rosettes of heart-shaped leaves and starry yellow flowers in spring. Stems grow from bulbils. Favours shady and moist conditions.
● Needs several treatments of lawn weedkiller.

Lesser trefoil (*Trifolium dubium*)
Patch-forming annual weed with trifoliate leaves and small yellow clover-like flowers. Favours alkaline soils.
● Needs one or two lawn weedkiller applications.

Mouse-ear chickweed (*Cerastium holosteoides*)
Mat-former with small oval hairy leaves and tiny white flowers. Grows anywhere.
● Killed with one application of lawn weedkiller.

Mouse-ear hawkweed (*Hieracium pilosella*)
This is not one of the serious weeds of lawns, but nevertheless may be found in some areas, especially where there is light, acid, sandy soils. The yellow

flowers are rather like those of the dandelion, but there the similarity stops. This hawkweed spreads by means of creeping stems, which grow from the rosette of leaves, rooting into the soil as they go. The leaves are oval and very hairy.
● Easily controlled by a single application of lawn weedkiller.

Parsley piert (*Aphanes arvensis*)
A small mat-forming annual with lobed, toothed leaves and minute, green, petal-less flowers.
● Control (not easy) with one or two applications of lawn weedkiller.

Plantains (*Plantago* species)
Rosette-forming weeds with large, broad or lanceolate leaves and poker-like spikes of green or brown flowers.
● Easily killed with lawn weedkiller (overall or spot treatment). Hand weeding for single plants.

Selfheal (*Prunella vulgaris*)
A creeping, mat-forming weed with oval leaves and heads of purple flowers.
● Two applications of lawn weedkiller should eradicate it.

Sheep's sorrel (*Rumex acetosella*)
Common on acid and sandy soils. Of creeping habit, it has arrow-shaped leaves and erect spikes of tiny green flowers which change to red.
● Two applications of lawn weedkiller usually eradicate this weed.

Smooth hawk's-beard (*Crepis capillaris*)
This is not too common but it can become established in lawns, particularly in areas with light sandy soils. It is drought tolerant and can therefore survive dry conditions. It can be mistaken for a dandelion, as the leaves are similar and carried in a rosette. However, the yellow flowers are produced in a branching flower stem. Like the

dandelion, it also has a deep, thick taproot.
● Control individual plants by hand weeding or spot treatment with weedkiller. Or give an overall application of weedkiller. Generally two applications are needed.

Speedwell (*Veronica chamaedrys*)
A spreading, patch-forming weed with tiny oval, toothed leaves and rounded blue flowers.
● Usually two applications of weedkiller are needed to control this weed.

Stemless thistle (*Cirsium acaule*)
This is also known as the dwarf thistle and is not regarded as a serious weed in lawns, but it may appear in areas with alkaline or limy soils. It forms a rosette of extremely prickly lanceolate leaves. The rather attractive reddish-purple flower head is stemless.
● Single plants can be removed by hand or spot treated with weedkiller. Alternatively give an overall application of weedkiller, two doses generally being required to eradicate this weed.

CONTROL OF BROAD-LEAVED WEEDS

Broad-leaved weeds are much less trouble in a well-cared-for lawn than in a neglected one, as the turf will be dense, therefore allowing less opportunity for weeds to establish. The neglected lawn, with its thin and patchy grass, provides little competition for weeds and so they quickly establish and spread.

Regular lawn care like mowing, feeding, watering and scarifying will ensure the desired dense sward.

◄ Drought-tolerant white clover, *Trifolium repens*, is a rampant weed capable of colonizing large areas.

► Annual meadow grass, *Poa annua*, is a common lawn weed and quickly takes over thin lawns. It can be controlled by maintaining a dense, healthy sward.

Overall application of weedkillers

If the lawn is badly infested with weeds, then the whole area should be treated with a lawn weedkiller. The best time for treatment is in spring, but early autumn is also another suitable period. Weedkiller may also be applied in summer, provided conditions are suitable. Bear in mind that the grass should be growing vigorously.

When applying weedkillers the soil should be moist – never use them during a drought. Also, ideally, the weather should be fine and warm.

For optimum control of a wide range of weeds, choose a lawn weedkiller that contains several active ingredients. The usual ones found in lawn weedkillers today are mecoprop, dicamba, 2,4-D, dichlorprop and MCPA.

A very popular method of weed control in use today is to apply a combined lawn fertilizer and weedkiller (some also contain ferrous sulphate to kill moss).

Granular formulations are best applied with a lawn fertilizer distributor. Liquid formulations should be applied by watering-can, fitted with a dribble bar (Fig. 21), or by sprayer.

For some weeds, a single application of weedkiller is not enough to completely eradicate them, and so a second dose may be needed about six weeks later.

Do remember that weedkillers and fertilizers *must* be used according to the manufacturers' instructions, the lawn may be damaged or the application may not be effective.

Fig. 21 The even application of liquid lawn weedkillers can be achieved by fitting a dribble bar to the watering can.

Fig. 22 Treatment of isolated weeds.

(a) Spot weeders in the form of an aerosol can are ideal for treating isolated weeds in a lawn, especially those with a rosette-forming habit of growth.

(b) The daisy grubber is equally useful, lifting isolated weeds out, complete with roots.

Spot treatment

If there are only a few isolated weeds, especially those with a rosette-forming habit of growth such as dandelion, daisies and plantains, then there is no need to apply weedkiller to the whole lawn. Instead the weeds can be treated individually and this is known as spot treatment.

There are available special 'spot weeders', for instance in the form of an aerosol can containing the chemicals 2,4-D and dicamba. The centre of each weed is given a quick spray (Fig. 22a).

Other spot weeders come in the form of a solid 'stick' which is impregnated with lawn weedkiller. Again the centre of the weed is treated.

Hand weeding

Hand weeding is practical only if there are a few isolated weeds in the lawn. The rosette-forming kinds like dandelions and plantains are the easiest to remove by hand, but small patches of spreading or mat-forming kinds can also be successfully controlled in this way.

With some lawn weeds, such as dandelions, it is important to remove all the roots as new plants can be produced from portions of root remaining in the soil. Remember that some have long taproots, such as dandelions, so you may have to dig down deeply to remove all the root.

There is a special tool, called a daisy grubber, for removing lawn weeds. It is something like a hand fork, except that it has only two prongs. The prongs are inserted into the ground under the weed (on each side of its stem) and the daisy grubber is then lifted to ease out the weed (Fig. 22b). It is well worth investing in one.

If you are unable to find a daisy grubber in garden centres or shops, then a narrow-bladed hand trowel would be perfectly suitable for removing lawn weeds. In this instance, however, more of the lawn would be disturbed.

If the removal of individual weeds by hand leaves holes in the lawn (this is more likely to happen when using a hand trowel), these should be filled with fine good-quality soil and the areas sown with grass seed.

Possibly coming under the heading of hand weeding is raking the lawn prior to mowing to raise up the stems of mat-forming weeds like white clover and yarrow, to expose them to the mower blades. Mowing off the stems helps to weaken lawn weeds.

WEED GRASSES

Weed grasses cause unsightly coarse patches in lawns and compete with the finer lawn grasses for foods and moisture. If not controlled, they will spread and eventually take over the lawn grasses. First, though, one needs to identify these grasses. The following are the most likely to invade lawns.

Annual meadow grass (*Poa annua*)
This is a very common weed and crops up all over the garden, being particularly troublesome in beds and borders. It will also establish in lawns, particularly if there are any thin patches, and will gradually take over.

This weed is low growing in habit, generally around 5 cm (2 in) high in lawns, somewhat tufted, with flat leaves of a light green colour, wrinkled when young. It is not as conspicuous in lawns as some other weed grasses and indeed blends fairly well into utility lawns that contain ryegrass. The branched flower heads are triangular in shape and whitish green. This annual grass seeds itself very freely.

Annual meadow grass can succumb to drought in summer and die, leaving bare patches in the lawn.

Cocksfoot (*Dactylis glomerata*)
A tufted, coarse, hairless perennial grass with flat leaves that have slightly rough edges. This very common grass does not flower in closely mown lawns.

Creeping soft grass (*Holcus mollis*)
This is a perennial grass related to Yorkshire fog, but is more slender and greener than that species. It has a creeping habit of growth and favours acid or lime-free soils.

Wall barley (*Hordeum murinum*)
An annual grass that sometimes becomes a weed in lawns, particularly in seaside areas. Of tufted habit, it has coarse, light green leaves and produces spikes of green flowers, but not usually when growing in lawns.

Yorkshire fog (*Holcus lanatus*)
This tufted perennial grass has soft downy grey-green leaves which really are conspicuous in ornamental lawns. The branched flower heads are pinkish or whitish but are not produced in lawns.

CONTROL OF WEED GRASSES

Weed grasses are not as easy to control as broad-leaved weeds, for obviously they are not affected by lawn weedkillers. There are various ways of controlling them, though.

● Good and regular lawn care is recommended as this ensures dense turf which weed grasses will find difficult to invade.

- Patches of weed grasses should be slashed with a knife to weaken them – slash through the leaves and the roots. Repeat this operation until the patches have been eradicated.

- The grass should be raked up before mowing to expose the leaves of the weed grasses to the mower, which will have a weakening effect.

- If the patches of weed grasses are quite large, they should be dug out, making sure the roots are removed. The holes should then be filled in with fresh soil and sown with grass seed.

MOSS, ALGAE AND LICHENS

- *Moss* Together with broad-leaved weeds, moss is the commonest invader of lawns. It will quickly colonize the lawn if the soil is poor, if the ground suffers from poor drainage and/or poor aeration, if the lawn is heavily shaded, and if it is regularly mown too closely, all of which result in thin, weak grass. Moss will quickly fill the spaces. It can spread rapidly in moist periods during autumn or spring and is probably more of a problem if the soil is acid or lime-free, as moss relishes this condition.

Obviously, then, the way to help prevent moss invasion is to rectify all of the above faults. If the soil is extremely acid, below pH 5.5 (ascertained by carrying out a soil test), apply ground limestone in autumn at the rate of 56 g per sq m (2 oz per sq yd).

If moss is found in lawns despite taking all precautions to prevent colonization, you will have to use a mosskiller to kill it off. The usual periods to use mosskillers are spring or early autumn.

Combined fertilizer and mosskiller enables you to do two jobs in one. There is one for spring and summer use and another for autumn. These are granular and most easily applied with a fertilizer spreader. They contain ferrous sulphate to kill moss. Lawn sand is a traditional mosskiller, also containing ferrous sulphate, and it can be applied evenly by hand.

Other mosskillers, containing dichlorophen, come in spray containers and are ideal for treating small areas. Others, with the active ingredients chloroxuron and ferric sulphate, plus nitrogen to green up the grass, are mixed with water and applied by watering-can fitted with a dribble bar.

When the moss has turned black, indicating it is dead, it should be raked out by the vigorous use of a spring-tine lawn rake; or a motorized scarifier can be used on large lawns. On no account attempt to rake out live moss as this will spread it and make matters even worse.

- *Algae* may appear in lawns that are in shade and have moist soil. They are primitive simple plants which create black slippery patches. Patches of algae can be eradicated with a lawn mosskiller or lawn sand (see above). Aerating and topdressing in autumn, as described in the previous chapter, will help to prevent algae from becoming established.

- *Lichens* are also primitive plants that may appear in shady lawns, particularly under trees. They consist of a combination of an alga and a fungus, which live together in mutual harmony. The most common lichen consists of leaf-like growths which are brownish or blackish when moist, but greyish when dry, when the 'leaves' also curl to reveal their undersides, which are white in colour.

Lichens are not particularly serious on lawns. They may, however, invade sparse turf resulting from poor growing conditions and drainage. To keep lichens at bay, these conditions should be improved. Lichens can be eradicated with lawn sand or lawn mosskiller (see above).

◄ **Moss will quickly colonize a lawn if the grass is weak and thin. Good lawn management helps prevent it establishing.**

· 5 ·

Unwelcome Visitors

Pests and diseases of plants are the bane of the gardener's life and often much time and money is spent keeping them under control. Lawns are certainly not immune to such troubles, though you will be happy to know that they suffer from relatively few.

Some lawn pests are common to various parts of the world, particularly earthworms which are considered among the major pests of lawns as they create many little piles of soil (wormcasts) on the surface. They do not directly harm the grass as they feed on decaying organic matter. Grubs or larvae of various beetles are quite common in some countries and cause damage by feeding on the roots of grasses.

Also an underground pest is the mole cricket which can be a serious invader of lawns in warm climates. This is a fascinating creature which lives in burrows in moist soil, its diet including roots and stems of plants. It resembles a mole because its front legs have been adapted for digging through the soil.

Most of the pests that are found in lawns do in fact live underground and feed off the roots of the grasses. Often they are the grubs or larval stages of various insects. The mole, though, a delightful little mammal, does not feed on grass but on earthworms. However, it is not doing the gardener a favour by keeping worms under control, for its burrowing activities cause real problems in lawns, resulting in subsidence and large heaps of soil (molehills) on the surface.

There are numerous fungal diseases that can attack lawns and some are found in various parts of the world, such as dollar spot and fusarium patch or snow mould, which are considered the major diseases.

Various mammals, including dogs, can do damage to lawns by disturbing the surface (the urine of bitches causes unsightly brown patches). Certain birds also fall into this category.

Then there are various disorders affecting lawns, like overdoses of fertilizer or weedkiller, drought, and frost damage.

Here, then, are the commonly found pests, diseases and disorders of lawns described in detail, together with methods, both chemical and manual, of preventing and/or eradicating them. It is hoped you do not have them all in your lawn!

PESTS

Among the major and some minor pests of lawns, the majority are insects, but there are a few exceptions, such as earthworms, and some mammals and birds.

Ants (*Larius* spp.)
These insects are found in various parts of the garden, favouring warm dry areas in which to make

their nests. Lawns are often included in their choice of nesting site. Ants also favour light sandy soils. They do not directly damage grass by eating it – although roots can be disturbed, which leads to the leaves of the grass becoming yellow – but they create little mounds of fine soil which are a nuisance, particularly when mowing, and they look unsightly.

Ants are active during the summer, particularly during hot weather. There are various types of ants that may be found in lawns, including yellow species.

● Before you start mowing the lawn the anthills are best dispersed with a stiff broom or besom. For the control of ants, use an ant killer or other pest killer which is suitable for lawns. Ant killers in powder form containing the active ingredient phoxim would be suitable. The powder can be shaken around the nests, and if desired watered in to kill pests below ground. A liquid insecticide containing carbaryl would also control ants. This can be applied by watering-can. Use it only when the soil is moist.

Bees – mining (*Andrena* spp.)

Like ants, mining bees create little mounds of soil on the surface of lawns during the process of nest making. They also favour other parts of the garden, such as under pathways and rocks. To avoid mistaking the bee's heap of soil for an anthill, take a close look at it: there should be a small hole in the top. Do not worry about getting near to these bees, as they do not sting.

Mining bees are not serious pests of lawns, although in some areas there may be quite large colonies.

● Before mowing, the little conical mounds of soil should be scattered with a stiff broom or besom. If the bees are present in sufficient numbers to warrant some sort of control measure, then scatter a powder insecticide containing gamma-HCH around and over the mound.

Chafer grubs

These grubs are the larvae of various chafers, which are fat, heavy beetle-like insects, and they feed on the roots of grass (Fig. 23). The adults do no direct harm to lawns.

The larvae of the garden chafer (*Phyllopertha horticola*) are those most likely to be found in lawns. This insect has the alternative name of June bug, for in the northern hemisphere it is quite active at that time of the year. The large brown adult insects lay their eggs in lawns and the resultant larvae feed on the roots of the grass during the spring and summer. This causes the grass immediately above to turn brown and die. A good test to discover whether or not chafer grubs are at work is to pull the dead grass. If the roots have been eaten the leaves are easily pulled up. The larvae of the garden chafer are large, fat, curved grubs, cream-white in colour, with six legs, and they have a shiny brown head. They take two years to mature. Other chafer grubs are similar, but vary in size.

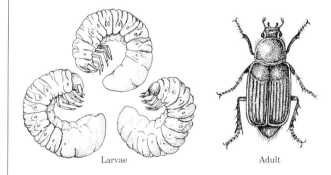

Larvae   Adult

Fig. 23 **Chafer grubs are the larvae of various chafers, such as the garden chafer. The grubs feed on the roots of grass but the adults do no direct harm to lawns.**

◀ Wormcasts are little mounds of wet sticky soil which render an ornamental lawn unsightly.

▶ Ants' nests often appear in lawns during the summer. These mounds of soil look unsightly and interfere with mowing.

Birds are partial to chafer grubs and they may cause secondary damage to lawns in their search for them. It is desirable, therefore, to take measures to control chafer grubs in lawns.
● A liquid pesticide containing carbaryl applied with a watering-can will eradicate the grubs. Apply it in spring or summer when the pests are active. The soil should be moist at the time of application.

Cutworms

These are the caterpillars or larvae of various night-flying moths, such as the large yellow underwing (*Noctua pronuba*) and they live in the soil and feed by cutting through the bases of stems, hence their common name. They also feed on the roots of plants (Fig. 24). Cutworms are occasionally found in lawns and are more of a problem in some countries than in others. Parts of Northern Europe, for instance, may experience severe damage from cutworms. An infestation may cause quite a lot of damage, eventually causing the grass to die off in patches.

The moths lay their eggs in late summer and the resulting larvae, which are usually green or grey-brown in colour, feed in the autumn, hibernate in the winter when the weather turns cold, and

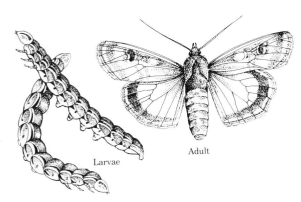

Fig. 24 Cutworms, which feed on stem bases and roots of plants, are the larvae of various night-flying moths, such as the large yellow underwing.

resume their feeding when conditions warm up again in the spring.

● Control of cutworms in lawns can be achieved by applying a dust insecticide containing gamma-HCH. Use it when the cutworms are active, in the autumn or in spring and summer.

Earthworms (*Allolobothora* spp.)

Gardeners are forever debating the pros and cons of earthworms in lawns (Fig. 25). The fact is that earthworms are beneficial to the soil, they do not harm plants but live on decaying organic matter. They help to aerate the soil during their burrowing, and they pull organic matter down into the soil. To summarize, they go a long way towards ensuring a healthy fertile soil.

So why are earthworms considered major pests of lawns? For the simple reason that during the course of their activities, some species throw up little mounds of wet sticky soil, popularly referred to as wormcasts.

In beds and borders, wormcasts are hardly noticeable, but they really show up on lawns and, without doubt, they look unsightly. Also, they are likely to be flattened during mowing. When this happens you are left with little muddy patches all over the lawn, which can in fact smother grass and at the same time encourage weed seeds to germinate.

Many gardeners, therefore, eradicate worms in their lawns, especially if they have fine ornamental lawns. Other gardeners may not worry, particularly if they have a utility lawn. Really it is up to the individual concerned whether or not worm control is to be undertaken.

Certainly before mowing, wormcasts should be scattered with a besom or stiff broom, to prevent them becoming flattened and turning into muddy patches.

Earthworms are found in lawns in many countries and various species are involved in cast-making. They favour moisture-retentive and humus-rich soils, as opposed to thin stony, gravelly, chalky or sandy types. The worms are most likely to make casts in the autumn or spring during moist and mild weather.

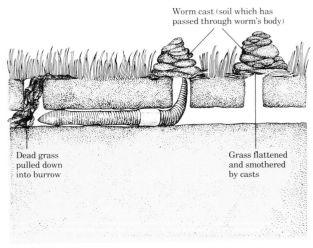

Worm cast (soil which has passed through worm's body)

Dead grass pulled down into burrow

Grass flattened and smothered by casts

Fig. 25 Earthworms aerate the soil and pull dead organic matter down into it but eject piles of sticky soil.

• HANDY TIP •

How do you know when leatherjackets are present in a lawn? A tell-tale sign is flocks of starlings feeding on the lawn. They are after the grubs. A reliable test is to drench a small part of the lawn with water, and then cover it with hessian or burlap. Leave this in place over night. If there are leatherjackets present, they will rise to the surface.

Help to deter earthworms by removing clippings during mowing. This reduces the amount of organic matter on the lawn surface. Increasing soil acidity also helps to deter worms: use acid fertilizers, do not apply lime and give an annual topdressing of peat. Do not apply topdressing mixtures that contain lime.

● Worms can be killed by treating lawns with a liquid pesticide containing the active ingredient carbaryl. This should be diluted according to the manufacturer's instructions and then applied with a watering-can. Use it during a mild, showery spell during spring or autumn, when the worms are active. The soil should be moist at the time of application, and the lawn should be mown beforehand.

Sweep up any worms that appear on the surface after treatment. Most, however, remain in the soil.

Fly larvae (*Dilophus* and *Bibio* spp.)

The larvae or grubs of various two-winged flies may sometimes appear in lawns. The adults are hairy black flies which live on organic matter like compost heaps. The grey-brown grubs are found in the autumn or spring in lawns: groups of them in nests just below the surface of the soil. They are sometimes mistaken for leatherjackets, but unlike leatherjackets the fly grubs have brown shiny heads (Fig. 26).

Fly larvae are not considered very important and are certainly not as destructive as leatherjackets. They feed mainly on rotting organic matter in the soil. Large numbers of grubs, though, disturb the grass around the nests and this has an adverse effect on growth.

● A liquid lawn pesticide containing carbaryl can be used to eradicate fly larvae. A single nest can be dug out with a trowel, the hole filled in with fresh soil and then re-seeded, if you do not want to use chemicals for control.

Leatherjackets (*Tipula* spp.)

These are the most serious insect pests of lawns. As well as occurring extensively in Britain, they can be a great problem in other parts of northern Europe.

They are the larvae of crane flies or daddy-longlegs, familiar two-winged flies with very long

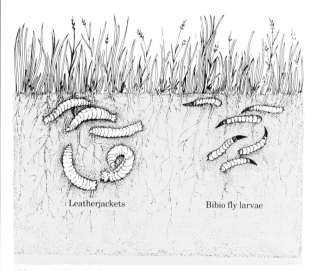

Fig. 26 Bibio fly larvae are often mistaken for the more serious leatherjackets or crane-fly larvae.

◀ Molehills are the lawn owner's nightmare. The burrowing activities of moles can eventually lead to subsidence of the lawn and an uneven surface.

▶ Leatherjackets are the larvae of crane flies or daddy-longlegs. They are serious pests, feeding on the roots of grass which results in yellow patches.

legs. The larvae or grubs are grey in colour and feed on roots and bases of stems of the grass. Eggs are laid by the adult flies in late summer and they hatch in the autumn. The larvae feed during the autumn and winter (Fig. 26).

The result of leatherjackets feeding on grass roots becomes apparent in the summer of the following year when the turf turns yellow in patches. The patches are particularly conspicuous when the lawn starts to become dry.

Try to deter leatherjackets by ensuring the lawn is well drained. Aeration will help to ensure this.

● When leatherjackets are present the lawn should be treated with a liquid insecticide (one that is suitable for lawns) containing carbaryl. Use it in the autumn when the pests are particularly active. Apply with a watering-can fitted with a dribble bar.

MAMMALS AND BIRDS

Birds

Surprisingly, our feathered friends can cause some damage to lawns, although they do not constitute a major problem.

During their search for grubs, especially leatherjackets (the larvae of crane flies), starlings will sometimes pull up tufts of grass.

Most trouble from birds is experienced on the new lawn site after sowing grass seed. Birds, especially

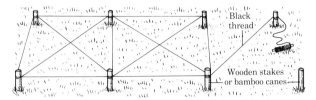

Fig. 27 To prevent birds from disturbing newly sown grass seed, stretch black thread over the site.

sparrows, may disturb the seeds as they have dust baths.

● Eliminate bird-attracting grubs in the lawn by using a lawn-pest killer. Ensure grass seed is treated with a bird repellent. Place brushwood over a newly sown lawn site, or stretch black thread over it in a criss-cross pattern (Fig. 27).

Dogs
Our four-legged friends are capable of doing quite a lot of damage to lawns. They may scratch up the grass, which is extremely damaging and not easily rectified. The urine of bitches scorches grass,

resulting in brown patches. Around each patch, the grass grows vigorously and is a rich green colour.

● The least amount of damage is caused by bitch urine if the grass is heavily watered immediately after the act has taken place.

Any areas that have been scratched up will have to be re-seeded after suitable preparation. Areas that have been scorched by urine should be watered heavily. If they do not recover, re-seeding or re-turfing is the only answer.

Moles (*Talpa europaea*)
The mole is a small mammal with soft black fur, that burrows in the soil with its very powerful front feet in its search for earthworms that are its staple diet. Moles form a network of tunnels, into which the worms drop (Fig. 28).

The damage caused in a lawn is heartbreaking. During the course of burrowing, the moles throw up

Fig. 28 Moles create burrows at different depths. The shallow ones, and the heaps of soil, damage lawns.

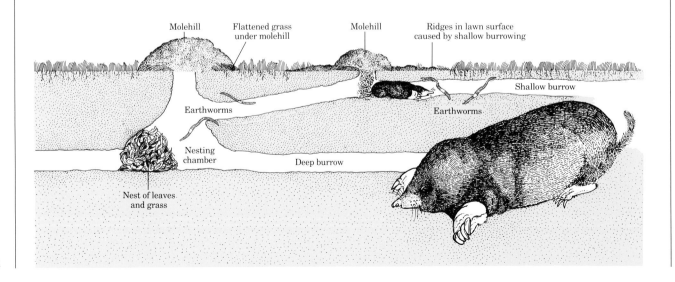

large mounds of soil, known as molehills. Their burrowing can also lead eventually to subsidence, especially on light soils, and an uneven surface. Shallow runs made just below the surface result in ridges in the lawn.

● To deter moles, ensure the lawn is free from earthworms. Mole traps can be placed in the burrows. There are various kinds available, suited to shallow and deep runs. When placing them, disturb the runs as little as possible and make sure no light enters by covering the area with layers of hessian or burlap. Mole smokes can be used, the active ingredient being sulphur. After flattening the molehills the cartridges are lit and inserted in the runs, then the holes are covered with soil.

DISEASES

The major and some less serious diseases are described in detail here, with their methods of control. Physiological disorders are also covered, plus how to cure the symptoms and prevent them occurring again.

Damping off (*Fusarium* spp. *Pythium* spp. and others)
This is a disease of seedlings that causes them to turn yellow and suddenly collapse and die. It generally occurs when grass seed has been sown too thickly and the seedlings are therefore very dense.
● To prevent damping off spreading, water the area affected and its surrounds with a copper fungicide.

Dollar spot (*Sclerotinia homoeocarpa*)
This is a widespread and serious disease of fine ornamental lawns, appearing mainly during late summer, although it is liable to crop up at other times, too. The disease is most likely to appear when the weather is humid.

The symptoms are unmistakable: pale yellow or golden-brown circular patches, varying from 2.5–5 cm (1–2 in) in diameter. If the disease is very severe, the circles may merge into each other to form one large patch.

Dollar spot is troublesome on lawns made up of fine grasses, such as creeping red fescue; utility lawns which contain coarser kinds are not troubled.

● A suitable fungicide containing carbendazim, benomyl or thiophanate-methyl should be applied to the lawn to control dollar spot. Use strictly according to the maker's instructions.

You should also encourage the grass to grow more strongly by applying sulphate of ammonia, a nitrogenous fertilizer, during the spring and summer. This should be well watered into the lawn.

Other ways to help prevent dollar spot from attacking your lawn are to carry out spiking during the autumn to improve aeration and drainage, and to scarify in autumn to remove thatch or dead grass.

Fairy rings (*Marasmius oreades* and others)
Fairy rings are produced in lawns by various fungi that live in the soil, the prime one being *Marasmius oreades* (Fig. 29).

The symptoms often appear as rings of lush deep green grass. There may be one or several rings. In

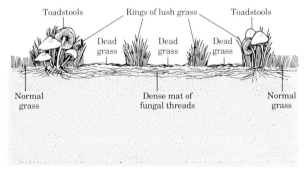

Fig. 29 Cross-section of a fairy ring produced by the fungus *Marasmius oreades*.

◀Red thread disease, *Corticium fuciforme.* Affected grass becomes bleached and later these areas are flushed with pink. The fungus produces pink horn-like growths.

▶ Fairy ring (*Marasmius oreades*). This fungal disease is unmistakable as it produces rings of toadstools in the lawn. It is not easy to control.

moist conditions during the summer and autumn, toadstools or puffballs are produced, also in rings. The symptoms differ slightly according to the fungus involved. With some, just the toadstools are produced without the ring of lush, deep green grass. Then with other fungi, one ring of such grass is produced.

With the most usual fungus, *Marasmius oreades*, the rings consist of an outside zone of lush deep green grass, a similar inside zone, and between them a zone of brown dead grass, or bare soil where the grass has long since died. The ring may be quite small, or it may be huge and virtually cover the whole lawn.

Marasmius oreades ramifies the soil with fungal threads, which form a very dense mat that goes down to a depth of 23 cm (9 in), but sometimes it extends to a staggering depth of 45 cm (18 in). These fungal threads indirectly cause the grass to die as described above, for they prevent moisture from reaching the grass roots. The grass, in fact, dies from drought and starvation – not by the direct action of the fungus.

There is no easy way of controlling fairy rings. If the fungus is already established, you should aim to prevent it from infecting other parts of the lawn. The toadstools or puffballs should be gathered up and burnt to prevent them from distributing their spores. The area should be mown separately from the rest of the lawn and the clippings burnt. The mower will have to be sterilized afterwards with a garden disinfectant.

● There is no chemical that will easily eradicate fairy rings, especially those produced by *Marasmius oreades*. However, some fungicides containing dichlorophen, provided they are suitable for application to lawns, can be tried. Follow the manufacturer's directions on use.

Another method of control is to dig up the turf to at least 30 cm (12 in) beyond the outer zone and to discard it. The soil can then be dug out to a depth of about 30 cm (12 in) and again discarded – ideally outside the garden in both cases. Refill the hole with fresh soil.

Fusarium patch (*Micronectriella nivalis*, syn. *Fusarium nivale*)
This fungal disease is widespread, being found in various parts of the world including the USA, Canada and Europe, and is considered to be one of the major lawn diseases.

The other common name for this disease is snow mould, the name used in America, since it may appear after a fall of snow, developing underneath the layer, especially where people have been walking on the lawn.

Fusarium patch appears mainly in the spring and autumn, though, and favours mild, damp weather. Symptoms start as little patches of yellow grass, of random shape. In severe attacks the patches may join together. The affected grass eventually becomes brown and then dies. During moist weather each patch may be surrounded by cotton-wool-like fungal growths, either white or light pink in colour.

Conditions which encourage fusarium patch include poor aeration; therefore pay attention to spiking in the autumn. Feeding during late summer with a high-nitrogen fertilizer may also encourage attacks of this disease. Avoiding this practice will help to discourage the disease, as will keeping the grass dry by brushing off dew in the mornings with a besom. Regular mowing to keep the grass short also helps to prevent the disease establishing, as air movement will be better. Do not walk on the lawn when it is covered with snow.

● To control fusarium patch water the lawn with a solution of fungicide containing carbendazim, thiophanate-methyl or benomyl.

Ophiobolus patch (*Gaeumannomyces graminis* var. *avenae*, syn. *Ophiobolus graminis* var. *avenae*)
Fortunately this is not a common fungal disease but where it does occur the symptoms are serious.

It appears during late sumer or autumn in the form of circular depressions of a pale yellow or

Fig. 30 The fungal disease ophiobolus patch appears as circular depressions in the lawn. The grass dies out and the depressions then become colonized by coarse grasses and weeds.

bronze colour. They are several centimetres (inches) in diameter.

The depressions gradually increase in size and a notable feature is that the centres, where the grass has been killed off, become colonized by coarse grasses and weeds (Fig. 30).

● Various soil conditions can encourage ophiobolus patch. It favours wet conditions, so pay attention if necessary to spiking in the autumn to ensure good drainage and aeration. It is more likely to occur on alkaline soils, so avoid liming the lawn and use acid topdressings.

Another way of helping to prevent this disease is to feed the lawn with the nitrogenous fertilizer sulphate of ammonia during the spring and summer.

The affected parts of the lawn should be re-turfed, after suitable preparation.

Red thread (*Corticium fuciforme*)

This fungal disease is commonly encountered and appears mainly during late summer and autumn, although it can crop up at any time of year.

Red thread is also known as corticium disease, and the symptoms are quite distinctive. The grass becomes bleached in patches, and later these areas become flushed with pink. During moist weather conditions the fungus produces pink horn-like branching growths among the grass stems and leaves, and later when they become brittle they are easily spread over the lawn by mower and feet. Red thread disease does not often kill the grass and indeed the bleached patches, if given suitable attention, usually recover.

Attacks of red thread are most common on lawns that suffer from poor aeration and fertility, especially if there is a shortage of nitrogen.

● To help prevent attacks, spike the lawn in autumn if necessary to ensure good aeration and drainage, and give dressings of the nitrogenous

· DISORDERS AFFECTING LAWNS ·

Cause	Symptoms	Prevention/cure
Drought	Generally the whole lawn or large parts of it turn brown; most likely time is late spring and summer	To prevent, water the lawn heavily each week before symptoms occur – best to spike or slit the lawn beforehand; the lawn will recover gradually at the onset of rain
Fertilizer scorch (too much applied or conditions too dry)	Grass turns brown or black in irregular patches with hand spreading; or in stripes or lines if a distributor was used, a few days after feeding	Never feed in dry conditions; water in fertilizer if no rain falls within two days; follow maker's instructions on use and never over-apply; avoid over-lapping when using distributor
Frost damage	This can occur if you walk on the lawn while it is covered in frost; black footmarks are the result and appear when the frost has thawed	Avoid walking on or otherwise using the lawn during frosty weather; no cure, but the bruised grass will eventually recover
Underground debris	The grass above buried rubbish can turn brown or yellow, especially during dry periods or drought	Remove all debris like bricks, lumps of concrete or stones during preparation of lawn site; lift turf, remove debris, add fresh soil to normal level then replace the turf
Weedkiller overdose	The grass turns brown and dies very soon after the application of lawn weedkiller	Follow the maker's instructions to the letter; in addition, avoid overlapping when applying in strips

◀Various kinds of toadstools may appear regularly in lawns and are generally harmless fungi which live on decaying wood in the soil.

▼ Scorching caused by excess fertilizer. To avoid this, always follow maker's instructions on use.

► Symptoms of drought. To avoid this, water the lawn heavily each week before symptoms occur – provided there is no ban on garden watering in your area.

fertilizer sulphate of ammonia during the spring and summer. Scarification in autumn to remove thatch also helps by ensuring good air circulation.

The fungus can be treated with suitable fungicides containing carbendazim, benomyl or thiophanate-methyl.

Toadstools (various fungi)

Various kinds of toadstools other than those already mentioned may appear regularly in lawns. There is no need to worry about these as they are the fruiting bodies of harmless fungi which live on decaying wood in the soil. The remedy is to lift the turf in the areas where the toadstools are growing, remove the woody debris and re-lay the turf.

● Toadstools are easily dispersed with a besom or stiff broom.

·6·
New Lease of Life

If not looked after on a regular basis, lawns soon deteriorate. There is possibly no worse sight in a garden than a neglected lawn, full of weeds, of a sickly looking colour and with patchy grass. It's the sort of thing that can happen when people move house. It is quite common to take over a house and garden to find that the lawn is in a state of neglect, perhaps with the grass 30 cm (1 ft) high! In another case, you may have no option but to neglect the lawn, and perhaps the garden in general, say if you are incapacitated for a long period.

But do not worry if you are confronted with such a sorry sight: it is not the end of the world and there is every chance the lawn can be brought back into tip-top condition without having to resort to creating a completely new lawn.

Of course, lawns also suffer from general wear and tear, which is another reason you may need to carry out repair work from time to time. The sort of things that can occur are broken edges. If these are left they create an air of general neglect, so should be put right as soon as possible.

The surface of a lawn may become uneven, resulting in hollows and bumps. These not only look unsightly, but they often make mowing difficult – mowers can completely slice off the grass from bumps, leaving bare soil. So these irregularities should also be seen to, at a suitable time of year.

For one reason or another bare patches – areas where the grass dies out – occur in lawns. You should first of all try to rectify the cause and then restore the grass either by sowing seed or laying turf.

All of these aspects of lawn care are covered in detail in this chapter. Let us hope you do not have to refer to it too often!

THE NEGLECTED LAWN

Although the lawn you are facing may be full of weeds and moss, of poor colour, and with patchy and perhaps very long grass, do not despair, for there is a good chance that it can be brought back to good condition. This is not always the case, though, and you will have to decide whether it would be better to kill off everything and create a new lawn on a clean site.

The first thing to do is carefully inspect the neglected lawn. If the perennial weeds such as clover, pearlwort and moss are so bad, and there is virtually no grass left, then it would be sensible to start from scratch. First kill everything off by spraying the area with a weedkiller containing glyphosate. Then follow the advice in Chapter 2 on site preparation and creating lawns from seed and turf.

However, as already indicated, all of this may not be necessary. If the lawn still consists mainly of the original grasses, rather than inundated with tufts of coarse grasses and broad-leaved weeds, then all that will be needed is a methodical maintenance programme. The best time to start this is in the spring, if possible.

If the grass is very long the first job will be to cut it down to a height of about 5 cm (2 in) (Fig. 31a). There are various ways of doing this: for small lawns use a bill hook, nylon-line trimmer or even garden shears. With a large lawn a powerful rotary mower would be more practical: consider hiring one for a weekend. The grass should be raked off and put on the compost heap.

Once the grass is shorter, have another close look at the lawn surface to ascertain what further problems need to be cured.

The next step is to rake the lawn vigorously to remove rubbish (Fig. 31b), and follow by brushing with a besom. Do not carry out scarification – which is very deep and severe raking – in the spring, as this is best done in autumn. It can, in fact, damage a lawn in spring.

From now on normal mowing can be carried out, but start off with the mower blades set at their maximum height as the lawn should not be mown closely at this stage. The height of cut should be lowered gradually over several weeks until the correct height for the type of lawn and time of year has been reached (see p. 42).

In the spring or early summer the weeds should be killed off with a lawn weedkiller, and likewise moss. The latter should be raked out when it has turned black, which indicates that it is dead. Full details on weed and moss control will be found in Chapter 4.

Next apply a lawn fertilizer formulated for spring and summer use. Details of fertilizers and their application are given in Chapter 3.

In the summer, carry out watering if necessary (provided there is no ban on garden watering) (Fig. 31c). Also you may feel that the grass needs a further boost, so give another application of

Fig. 31 Renovation of a neglected lawn.

(a) Cutting down long grass.

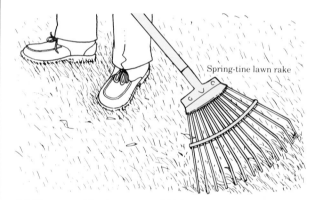

(b) Vigorous raking to remove rubbish.

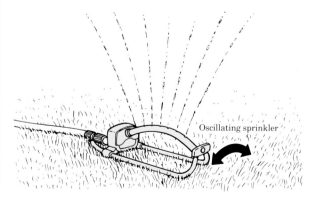

(c) Watering, especially after applying fertilizers.

◄Although this neglected lawn is fairly weedy, there is a good chance that it can be brought back to good condition by carrying out a methodical maintenance programme.

▶ A damaged lawn edge looks unsightly and gives a general air of neglect, yet it is so easily repaired in autumn, winter or early spring. An edging strip will prevent it.

fertilizer. You could use a liquid formulation at this time, as this will give a quick boost to growth.

Further maintenance tasks can be carried out in early autumn. Scarification to remove thatch or dead grass is one of the important jobs, especially on a neglected lawn – see Chapter 3.

Other essential autumn tasks will be aerating or spiking followed by topdressing, and the application of an autumn lawn fertilizer (see Chapter 3). It is likely that a worm killer will need to be applied, too, as described in Chapter 5.

It is also likely that various lawn repairs will be needed, which are discussed below, and these can be carried out later in the autumn when the essential maintenance tasks are completed.

From the following spring the normal yearly routine maintenance programme can be carried out – refer to Chapter 7 for timely reminders.

Fig. 32 Repairing a broken lawn edge.

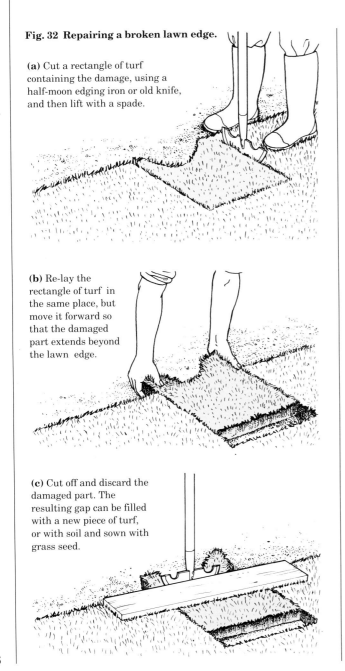

(a) Cut a rectangle of turf containing the damage, using a half-moon edging iron or old knife, and then lift with a spade.

(b) Re-lay the rectangle of turf in the same place, but move it forward so that the damaged part extends beyond the lawn edge.

(c) Cut off and discard the damaged part. The resulting gap can be filled with a new piece of turf, or with soil and sown with grass seed.

• HANDY TIP •

Where can one obtain finely sifted soil for filling cracks in relaid turf? The best bet for small areas is to buy a bag of loam from your local garden centre. For larger areas, use a topdressing mixture as described on page 51.

REPAIRS

As with most other parts of the garden, the lawn will occasionally need some repair work. The parts of the lawn most vulnerable to damage are the edges. The lawn may develop hollows and bumps, or bare patches.

Damaged edges

The best time to carry out repairs to lawn edges is in autumn, winter or early spring, as invariably some turf has to be lifted and relaid. At these times there is little risk of the newly laid turf drying out.

To repair a broken edge, cut out a rectangle of turf containing the damage. It is best cut with a half-moon edging iron. Alternatively, an old knife can be used. Lift the rectangle of turf with a spade: it should be about 2.5 cm (1 in) thick, with some soil attached (Fig. 32a). Now re-lay the rectangle in the same place, but move it forward so that the damaged part extends beyond the lawn edge, then cut it off and discard it (Fig. 32b). You will now be left with a gap. This can be filled with a new piece of turf if you have some available (Fig. 32c). If there are any cracks after laying, brush some fine soil into them. Alternatively the gap can be filled to the correct level with fine soil and sown with grass seed in the spring.

Occasionally lawn edges need re-cutting to smarten them up. Again use a half-moon edging iron and carry out the operation in the spring. A plank of wood can be used as a guide for straight edges, cutting hard against it with the iron. Never cut away too much, or do it too frequently, or you will soon make the lawn considerably smaller! The edges should be given a slight slope as this makes them more stable and less prone to damage.

Hollows and bumps

Hollows and bumps should also be attended to in autumn, winter or early spring as, again, turf generally needs to be lifted. Some people are tempted to flatten bumps with a garden roller, but this is not often successful and indeed is not advised as it can severely compact the soil. Never attempt to fill deep hollows with soil as this will only kill off the grass. However, shallow depressions can be dealt with in this way over a period of time, using finely sifted soil, but no more 12 mm ($^1/_2$ deep) at any one time. Work it well into the turf with a stiff brush.

For bumps and deep hollows turf will need to be lifted, so once again you will require a half-moon edging iron for cutting it, the alternative being an old knife. Lifting of the turf can be done with a spade.

With the edging iron or knife, cut the turf in a square or rectangle, extending slightly beyond the bump or hollow. Make another cut through the centre and then 'peel back' the turf rather than lift it completely (Fig. 33). Next add or remove soil as required. The soil should be trodden firm before replacing the turf. Firm the turf, then fill any gaps by brushing some finely sifted soil into them.

The above is for small bumps and hollows. For larger areas, you will need to lift an area of turf of the appropriate size completely.

Bare patches

Bare patches can be caused by various things, as mentioned throughout the book, such as scalping of bumps by the lawn mower; killing of the grass by diseases, overdoses of weedkiller and bitch urine;

Fig. 33 Curing small bumps and deep hollows in lawns.

(a) Lift the turf by cutting it in a square or rectangle, extending slightly beyond the bump or hollow, then make another cut through the centre.

(b) 'Peel back' the turf rather than lift it completely. Next add or remove soil as required, then replace the turf.

Bare patches can be re-seeded in spring or early autumn. It is possible to buy from garden centres small packets of grass seed specially for this purpose.

weed and moss eradication; general wear and tear; and overhanging plants. Generally you should aim to prevent bare patches occurring, but if they do appear follow the guidelines below on repairing them.

One has a choice of establishing new grass in bare patches by turfing or sowing grass seed. Full details on soil preparation, sowing grass seed and laying turf will be found in Chapter 2.

To returf small areas, which should be done in autumn, winter or spring, you should cut the turf in a square or rectangle, with an edging iron or knife, slightly larger than the bare soil, and lift it. The soil should then be broken up with a fork and firmed. New turves are then laid – it may be necessary to add or remove soil at this stage to ensure the turves are level with the rest of the lawn surface. Then firm them down and fill any cracks by brushing finely sifted soil into them.

Where does one obtain the small quantities of turf needed to repair bare patches? It is unlikely that you will be able to obtain small amounts from a specialist turf supplier, so you will have to find an alternative source of supply. Bearing in mind that it should contain the same grasses as the existing lawn to ensure that the repaired area is not conspicuous, one answer is to lift some turf from another part of the lawn where it will not be noticed too much. Then this area could be re-seeded (see below).

Another idea is to have a 'turf nursery' which contains the same grasses as those in the lawn. Indeed, any turf that is left over from making a new lawn could be grown in a 'nursery'.

The nursery does not have to be elaborate or extensive by any means. An odd corner of the vegetable or fruit plot could, perhaps, have a square of spare turf. Or why not have grass paths in the vegetable garden? You could then 'raid' these whenever some turf is required, and replace them by sowing grass seed.

It goes without saying that an area of spare turf needs the same high quality of maintenance as the lawn, otherwise it will soon deteriorate and be no good for repair work.

Re-seeding can be done in spring or early autumn. Before sowing, shallow fork over the bare patch with a garden or hand fork – no more than about 12 mm ($^1/_2$ in) deep. Then, using an iron rake, rake the soil down to a fine tilth and remove any rubbish. Sow the seed at a rate of 50 g per sq m ($1^1/_2$ oz per sq yd), then sift over a thin layer of fine soil just enough to cover it.

Remember that the grass-seed mixture used for re-seeding must contain the same kinds of grasses as in the original lawn, otherwise the re-sown areas may be quite conspicuous. For instance, never use a mixture intended for a utility lawn on a fine ornamental lawn, and *vice versa*.

If certain areas or parts of the lawn keep becoming bare, then something must be wrong and you may have to think about an alternative to replacing the grass. For instance, it might be quite impossible to permanently establish grass under a large tree which creates heavy shade. However, instead of having just bare soil, which may become invaded by moss, consider planting tough, drought-tolerant, shade-loving ground-cover plants below it. A selection has been given in Chapter 1.

Shrubs and other plants that encroach on to the lawn from adjacent borders and beds result in the grass dying out beneath them. It is a complete waste of time trying to re-establish grass in these areas. What is the solution? Certainly not cutting back the shrubs, as this often involves hard pruning which can ruin their shape. Instead, if the plants cannot be moved back, re-cut the edge of the lawn around them – in other words, extend the bed or border! In future, when planting, bear this point in mind and plant the shrubs or other plants sufficiently well back from the lawn. This means you will have to find out the ultimate spread of the plants.

The design of the garden may result in bare patches re-occurring in the same place on the lawn. For instance, if the lawn has only one access point this area may quickly become threadbare due to frequent use. In this instance you may find it better to have a paved entrance (brick paving looks good), making it fan out so that you can vary access to the lawn. Ideally, though, try to have several different places from which you can get onto the lawn.

Remember that the grass-seed mixture used for re-seeding bare patches must match the grasses in the existing lawn.

·7·
The Lawnsman's Calendar

Lawn care is a year-round task, there being very few periods when one can honestly say that there is nothing to do. Why is this? Well, grass grows for much of the year, even in winter (especially during mild spells), although growth is very much slower then. So, while the regular mowing season starts in early spring and finishes in mid-autumn, occasional lawn mowing may be needed in between.

Some seasons are quieter than others. Obviously winter is the slackest period, as it is in the rest of the garden. During this season one can take advantage of the lull in activities and carry out lawn repairs.

Winter is also the major period for creating a new lawn from turf. The period for laying turf actually runs from late autumn to early spring. Spring sees frenzied activity on the lawn! Apart from starting to mow the grass, we have to cut the lawn edges. It is also time to apply fertilizer to encourage vigorous growth of a good green colour, and to carry out a weed and moss control programme. Spring is also the major time for creating new lawns from seed, although this can be tackled in early autumn as well.

Summer sees the continuation of mowing, although this may be much reduced if there are periods of dry weather or drought when the grass is not growing. Also continuing will be edging, feeding if needed, and the application of weedkiller, but again only if necessary.

Autumn is an extremely important season as far as lawn care is concerned, as numerous tasks need to be carried out. This often comes as a surprise to many new gardeners. Important tasks include scarifying to remove dead grass, aeration to ensure good drainage and air penetration, topdressing to improve the soil, and the application of an autumn lawn fertilizer. Mosskiller, pesticides and fungicides may also need to be applied.

The accompanying chart (pp. 91–4) lists all lawn jobs season by season under the headings of 'Lawn preparation', 'Maintenance', 'Feeding and watering', and 'Pests, diseases, weeds'. These are all fully discussed in the preceding chapters and to make for easy reference appropriate page numbers have been given for each task in the chart.

Although it is important to carry out the various aspects of lawn care in the right season, remember that it is best to choose a time when soil and weather conditions are most suitable. Remember, too, that it may not be necessary to carry out all of these operations on your lawn. It is up to you to decide what needs to be done to keep your lawn looking good and in tip-top condition.

EARLY SPRING

Lawn preparation

Grass seed can be sown if soil and weather conditions are suitable (**p. 33**).

Lay turf. This is the last opportunity until early autumn (**p. 35**).

Grass seed and wild-flower mixture can be sown to create a wild-flower meadow (**p. 37**).

Re-seed bare patches (**p. 87**)

Maintenance

New grass can be mown for the first time when about 8 cm (3 in) high (**pp. 35-36**).

Lawn mowers and other equipment can be bought during this season. Shops should be well stocked (**p. 39**).

Begin mowing on a regular basis and continue until mid-autumn (**p. 42**).

Height of cut should be raised when mowing (**p. 43**).

Lawn edging starts now and continues until mid-autumn (**p. 47**).

Rake the lawn to clear up rubbish that has accumulated over the winter (**p. 48**).

Surface aeration can be carried out lightly throughout spring if needed (**p. 50**).

Lawn repairs, such as broken edges, hollows and bumps. Final opportunity (**p. 86**).

Feeding and watering

Lawn fertilizer can be applied now, using one formulated for spring and summer use (**p. 52**).

Feed non-grass lawns with a general-purpose fertilizer. Once a year is sufficient (**p. 54**).

Pests, diseases, weeds

Lawn weedkiller can be applied, making sure you follow maker's instructions on use (**p. 60**).

Mosskiller can be applied now if needed; rake out the moss when it is dead (it turns black). Mosskiller will also kill algae and lichens (**p. 65**).

Lawn pesticides can be applied to kill chafer grubs, cutworms and fly larvae. Pesticides can be applied through spring (**p. 66**).

Earthworm control, by applying a pesticide containing carbaryl (**p. 70**).

Fusarium patch control by applying a suitable fungicide. Can be applied at any time in spring (**p. 78**).

MID-SPRING

Lawn preparation

Grass seed can be sown if soil and weather conditions are suitable (**p. 33**).

Grass seed and wild-flower mixture can be sown to create a wild-flower meadow (**p. 37**).

Chamomile, thymes and mints can be planted to create non-grass lawns (**p. 38**).

Re-seed bare patches (**p. 87**).

Maintenance

New grass can be mown for the first time when about 8 cm (3 in) high (**pp. 35-36**).

Height of cut can be lowered from now on when mowing the lawn (**p. 43**).

Carry out occasional raking throughout spring to raise up creeping weeds and coarse grasses (**p. 48**).

Feeding and watering

Lawn fertilizer for spring and summer use can be applied now, if not done earlier (**p. 52**).

Watering may be needed now and throughout spring, provided there is no ban (**p. 53**).

Feed bulbs growing in grass with a liquid fertilizer to build them up for next year (**p. 54**).

Feed non-grass lawns with a general-purpose fertilizer if not done earlier (**p. 54**).

Pests, diseases, weeds

Perennial weeds can be killed on new lawn site between now and late summer, while they are in active growth (**p. 25**).

Lawn weedkiller can be applied if needed (**p. 60**).

Mosskiller can be applied if this was not done earlier (**p. 65**).

LATE SPRING

Lawn preparation	Maintenance	Feeding and watering	Pests, diseases, weeds
Grass seed can be sown now. Watering may be required to assist germination (**p. 33**).	New grass can be mown for the first time when it is about 8 cm (3 in) in height (**pp. 35-36**).	Lawn fertilizer formulated for spring and summer use can be applied now if not done earlier (**p. 52**).	Lawn weedkiller can be applied if needed (**p. 60**).
Chamomile, thymes and mints can be planted to create non-grass lawns (**p. 38**).	Height of cut can be lowered when mowing the lawn (**p. 43**).	Feed bulbs growing in grass with a liquid fertilizer to build them up for next year (**p. 54**).	Mosskiller can be applied if this was not done earlier (**p. 65**).
Bare patches can be re-seeded. Watering may be needed to assist germination (**p. 87**).	Scarify in moderation to remove dead moss (**p. 47**).		

EARLY SUMMER

Lawn preparation	Maintenance	Feeding and watering	Pests, diseases, weeds
Lawn preparation should have been completed by now.	Height of cut can be lowered when mowing the lawn (**p. 43**).	Liquid fertilizer can be applied if the lawn needs a boost to growth (**p. 56**).	Lawn weedkiller can be applied now and throughout summer if conditions are suitable (**p. 60**).
	Scarify in moderation to remove dead moss but avoid too vigorous raking (**p. 47**).	Watering may be needed throughout summer if there are dry spells or there is a drought, but do comply with any bans on watering (**p. 53**).	Ant killer may be needed if ants are nesting in the lawn (**p. 66**).
	Rake the lawn lightly and periodically throughout summer to raise up creeping weeds and coarse grasses (**p. 48**).		A pesticide suitable for lawns may need to be applied to kill chafer grubs and cutworms. It may be used throughout summer (**pp. 67-69**)
	Light surface aeration can be carried out now and throughout summer if considered necessary – say if the surface is becoming compacted through heavy use (**p. 50**).		
	Cut the grass where bulbs have been planted, but only if their leaves have completely died down (**p. 54**).		

MID-SUMMER

Lawn preparation	Maintenance	Feeding and watering	Pests, diseases, weeds
———	Lower height of cut when mowing. However, it may need to be raised during dry or drought conditions (**p. 43**).	Liquid fertilizer may be applied if you feel the lawn needs a boost to growth, but only if not done earlier (**p. 52**).	Ant killer may be needed if ants are nesting in the lawn (**p. 66**).

MID-SUMMER (continued)			
Lawn preparation	**Maintenance**	**Feeding and watering**	**Pests, diseases, weeds**
——	Scarify in moderation to remove dead moss (**p. 47**).	——	——
	Mow long-grass areas (or wild-flower meadows) and rake up the hay (**p. 54**).		

LATE SUMMER			
Lawn preparation	**Maintenance**	**Feeding and watering**	**Pests, diseases, weeds**
——	Lower height of cut when mowing, but not during dry or drought conditions when the grass is not growing (**p. 43**).	Liquid lawn fertilizer can be applied if you feel the lawn needs a boost, but only if it was not done earlier (**p. 52**).	Ant killer may be needed if ants are nesting in the lawn (**p. 66**).
	Scarify in moderation to remove dead moss (**p. 47**).		Fungicide suitable for lawn use may need to be applied to control the diseases dollar spot and red-thread (**pp. 75,79**).
	Lightly trim chamomile lawns with shears to maintain neat growth. Trim thyme and mint lawns to remove dead flowers (**p. 54**).		

EARLY AUTUMN			
Lawn preparation	**Maintenance**	**Feeding and watering**	**Pests, diseases, weeds**
Grass seed can be sown now (**p. 33**).	New grass can be mown for the first time about 8 cm (3 in) (**pp. 35-36**).	Topdressing can be applied after aeration, but not needed every year (**p. 51**).	Lawn weedkiller can be used if necessary (**p. 60**).
Turf can be laid from now onwards (**p. 35**).	Raise height of cut when mowing lawns from now onwards (**p. 43**).	Autumn lawn fertilizer can be applied now (**p. 52**).	Lawn mosskiller (also kills algae and lichens) can be used if necessary (**p. 65**).
Sow grass seed and wild-flower mixture to create a wild-flower meadow. This is the best time for sowing (**p. 37**).	Scarify to remove thatch (layer of dead grass) (**p. 47**).		Pesticides suitable for lawns can be used to kill cutworms, leatherjackets and fly larvae. Can be applied throughout autumn (**pp. 69,71**)
Plant spring-flowering bulbs in lawns (**p. 38**).	Carry out deep aeration only, once every three or so years (**p. 50**).		Use pesticide containing carbaryl to control earthworms (**p. 70**).
Bare patches can be re-seeded now (**p. 87**).	Mow long-grass areas (or wild-flower meadows) and rake off the hay (**p. 54**).		The diseases fusarium patch and red-thread can be controlled with a suitable fungicide (**pp. 78,79**).
	Lawn repairs, such as broken edges, and bumps and hollows (**p. 86**).		

MID TO LATE AUTUMN

Lawn preparation	Maintenance	Feeding and watering	Pests, diseases, weeds
Plant spring-flowering bulbs in lawns (**p. 38**). Prepare the site for a new lawn, this being an especially good time, before the ground becomes too wet and/or frozen (**p. 23**). Turf can be laid (**p. 35**).	This is the end of the regular mowing season but remember that occasional mowing may be needed in winter (**p. 42**). Height of cut should be raised from now on when mowing (**p. 43**). Lawn edging should not be needed until spring (**p. 47**). Carry out lawn repairs, such as broken edges, bumps and hollows (**p. 86**). Fallen leaves should be raked up to prevent the grass from being smothered and for the sake of a tidy appearance (**p. 48**). Mowers can be serviced during this quiet period, in readiness for the next mowing season (**p. 41**).	Autumn lawn fertilizer can be applied now if not done earlier (**p. 52**).	No further chemical control should be needed until next spring.

WINTER

Lawn preparation	Maintenance	Feeding and watering	Pests, diseases, weeds
Prepare site for new lawn before ground becomes too wet and/or frozen (**p. 23**). Turf can be laid, provided ground is in suitable condition (**p. 35**).	Mowing may be needed occasionally in winter if the grass is growing (**p. 42**). Height of cut should be raised when mowing (**p. 43**). Lawn repairs, such as attention to broken edges, bumps and hollows, can be carried out (**p. 86**). Mower servicing should be carried out (**p. 41**).	———	———

Index